CONTENTS

WHEN TO PRAY

WHAT TO PRAY FOR

OVER 200 QUESTIONS
CHILDREN ASK
ABOUT PRAYER, HEAVEN,
AND ANGELS

Over 200 Questions Children Ask about Prayer, Heaven, and Angels

General Editor:
Daryl J. Lucas

Contributors:
David R. Veerman, M.Div.
James C. Galvin, Ed.D.
James C. Wilhoit, Ph.D.
Bruce B. Barton, D.Min.
Richard Osborne
Jonathan Farrar

Illustrator:
Lil Crump

FAMILY
CHRISTIAN
PRESS

Visit Tyndale's exciting Web site at *www.tyndale.com*

Over 200 Questions Children Ask about Prayer, Heaven, and Angels contains material from the following previously published books:

107 Questions Children Ask about Prayer and *104 Questions Children Ask about Heaven and Angels,* produced for Tyndale House Publishers by Lightwave Publishing and The Livingstone Corporation. Bruce B. Barton, James C. Galvin, David R. Veerman, Daryl J. Lucas, Jonathan Farrar, Livingstone project staff.

ISBN 0-8423-4244-3

Printed in the United States of America

06 05 04 03 02 01 00
 7   6   5   4   3   2   1

INTRODUCTION

Children have lots of questions about prayer, heaven, and angels. We know. We collected hundreds before they turned off the spigot.

Some of their questions are easy to answer, such as "Can you fall out of heaven?" But many others strike at the heart of our ignorance. Haven't you ever heard a child ask, "Why can't I see Jesus now?" Hmm . . .

Easy responses to tough questions are "I don't know," "Just because," and "Because I said so!" Those may be responses, but they're not answers. And they certainly don't help the child sort truth from error.

That's why we wrote this book: to help you answer children's tough questions about prayer, heaven, and angels.

The questions come entirely from real children (with a little editing for clarity). We surveyed children ages three to twelve and collected their responses, then sorted them (the questions, not the children) until we identified over two hundred of the most common and important ones. If you are a parent or if you work with children very often, you will surely hear questions like these—if you haven't already!

The answers, however, come entirely from Scripture. For every question, we looked in the Bible for the most relevant passages, then summarized their application to that question. Take time to study the Scriptures listed because the Bible is our final authority. God's Word alone reveals what we know about these important topics.

As you answer children's questions, keep the following points in mind.

- "Silly" questions are serious questions. Always take children's questions seriously. Don't laugh at them. Some questions may sound silly to you, but they're not silly to your child. Be careful not to ridicule your child's imaginative ideas.
- Some questions hide fears or insecurities. For example, when a little girl asks, "Are all people nice in heaven?" she's asking about her own safety, not just heaven. She knows what bullies are like, and she's afraid of them. She wants assurance that in heaven no one will be mean to her or push her around. Go ahead and answer the question behind the question—assure your child that there are no bullies in heaven. If you suspect that there may be a hidden question but don't know what it is, a great way to get at it is to ask, "Why do you ask?" or "Why do you want to know?"
- The best answers come from Scripture. The Bible doesn't answer every curiosity we have, but it is our only authoritative source for information on heaven and angels. The best thing you can do to prepare to answer questions like these is to study the Scriptures yourself.
- The best answers avoid theological jargon. Use normal words. Children think in literal terms, so abstract concepts don't mean a thing to them. As much as possible, talk about *things, events,* and *objects* they can imagine. Describe a smell. Mention a thing. Talk about an action, such as running. Give them something to look at in their minds. If they can see it, they will understand it.
- Some questions have no answer. Be careful not to make up an answer when you don't have one and when the Bible is silent. If you don't have an answer,

say so. Or suggest that you look for the answer together. If you get in the habit of inventing answers, your children will later lump faith with stories and superstitions they've discovered were false. Emphasize the truths of Scripture that you *do* know.

- Some kids just want to keep asking. Be ready for follow-up questions, and be willing to keep talking. Your answer may lead to more questions. That's the mark of a good answer—it makes your child think.

We wrote this book to help you answer kids' questions about prayer, heaven, and angels. We sincerely hope and pray it does that.

—Dave Veerman, Jim Galvin, Jim Wilhoit, Bruce Barton, Daryl Lucas, Rick Osborne, Jon Farrar, Lil Crump

Q: WHAT IS PRAYER?

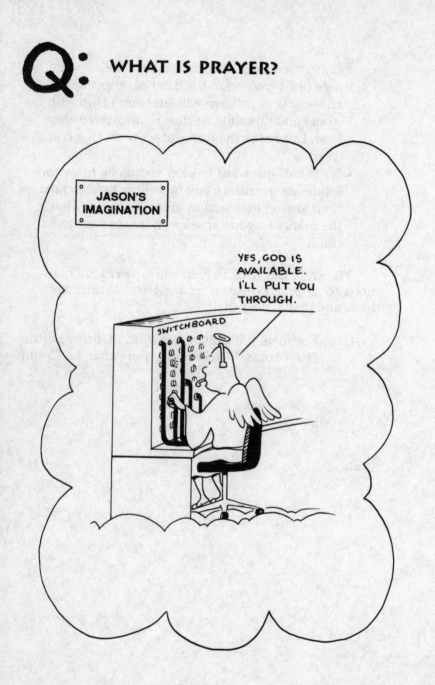

1

A: Prayer is the way we talk with God, just as conversation is the way we talk with our friends and parents. It is the way God has given us to thank him and to ask him to be involved in our lives.

Prayer is an important part of a friendship with God. Friends talk with each other a lot. It is the same with God and his friends. God's friends talk to him. They communicate. They pray.

KEY VERSE: *O God, listen to my prayer. Pay attention to my plea. (Psalm 54:2)*

RELATED VERSES: *Ephesians 2:18; Colossians 4:2; 1 Timothy 2:1; Revelation 8:3-4*

RELATED QUESTIONS: *Why is praying called praying? Who made prayer up?*

NOTE TO PARENTS: *Prayer is not a goal in itself. The goal is the relationship with God and all that comes with it. Help your children to understand this, and the process will be easier for them to grasp.*

Q: WHAT IS PRAYER FOR?

God's
Communication
station

2

A: The purpose of prayer is for us to get closer to God. When we tell God that we are sorry for our sins, thank him for all he has done, and ask for his help, God begins to change us. He changes our thoughts and desires, and he shows us what he wants us to do. We come to love him more and to see things from his point of view. Also, prayer gives us an opportunity to say, "Your will be done." It is a way for us to work with God to change the world. Think about it this way: God is our Father. He loves us and wants to meet our needs, to teach us how to live, to take care of us, and to use us. He wants to be our friend. Prayer asks him to do that in our lives. We pray because it invites our loving Father to work in our lives and in our world.

KEY VERSE: *You haven't done this before. Ask, using my name, and you will receive, and you will have abundant joy. (John 16:24)*

RELATED VERSES: *Psalms 4:1; 17:6; Philippians 4:6; James 5:16; 1 Peter 3:12*

RELATED QUESTIONS: *What's prayer supposed to be for? Is praying good?*

NOTE TO PARENTS: *Prayer is a lot like a conversation between a parent and a child. This analogy will help you explain prayer.*

Q: WHY DO WE HAVE TO PRAY INSTEAD OF JUST ASKING GOD?

3

A: Prayer does not have to be very formal and serious. Prayer can be natural, like having a talk with a friend. Whenever we have a need, we can just talk to God. We can tell him what we are excited about, tell him what worries us, or ask him for help. So when we pray, we *are* just asking God. We are talking to our best Friend.

We can pray about anything, anytime, anywhere, because God loves us.

KEY VERSE: *I prayed to the Lord, and he answered me, freeing me from all my fears. (Psalm 34:4)*

RELATED VERSES: *Philippians 4:6; 1 Thessalonians 5:17; 1 Timothy 2:1; Philemon 1:4*

RELATED QUESTIONS: *Why is prayer so complicated? When I pray, why does my mind wander? What's the meaning of prayer?*

NOTE TO PARENTS: *Prayer should be a very normal part of a child's life. The more conversational and real-life we make it, the easier it will be for children to understand. Prayer should not be so overly formalized that it becomes detached from the rest of their lives.*

Q: WHY DO WE HAVE TO PRAY TO GOD?

CHRISTIANS POWER UP THROUGH PRAYER LIKE A VACUUM CLEANER POWERS UP WHEN PLUGGED IN.

4

A: We have to pray to God because he is the only one who can answer. He is the only one who can give us what we need. And only God can satisfy our *deepest* needs—the needs we don't even know we have. God is everywhere and knows everything and can do anything, so he can hear everyone's prayers and answer them. Praying to ancestors, idols, angels, or people does not make sense because only God can answer prayer.

Praying to God is an awesome privilege. God made it so that we could get to know him, our heavenly Father, and have him care for us, teach us, and meet our needs. It's not a bad thing that we "have to pray." It's a good thing!

KEY VERSES: *Bend down, O Lord, and hear my prayer; answer me, for I need your help. Protect me, for I am devoted to you. Save me, for I serve you and trust you. You are my God. (Psalm 86:1-2)*

RELATED VERSES: *1 Kings 8:38-39, 60; Psalms 17:6; 32:6; 66:19-20; James 5:16*

RELATED QUESTIONS: *Why do people pray to God? Why do people say prayers?*

NOTE TO PARENTS: *Although prayer is to be an important part of our disciplined daily routine, we should always present it as an awesome privilege and encourage our children to see it that way. Making them pray or being stern about it won't give them a long-term desire to pray.*

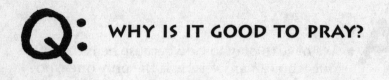

Q: WHY IS IT GOOD TO PRAY?

5

A: Praying is good because it brings us closer to God, our heavenly Father. Being a Christian means having a relationship with God. Prayer is a part of that relationship. Friends talk with each other, and God is our friend. Prayer makes our relationship with God better. We wouldn't have a very good relationship with him if we never talked to him.

It is also good to pray because God tells us to do it. All that God is and wants is good. Those who love God know this. They try to obey God and do what pleases him. So even though we may not always feel like praying, we should pray anyway because God says it is good to do. And if he says we should do it, then that is what is best for us and our lives.

KEY VERSES: *But you, dear friends, must continue to build your lives on the foundation of your holy faith. And continue to pray as you are directed by the Holy Spirit. Live in such a way that God's love can bless you as you wait for the eternal life that our Lord Jesus Christ in his mercy is going to give you. (Jude 1:20-21)*

RELATED VERSES: *Matthew 5:44; Luke 22:40, 46; 1 Timothy 2:1, 8*

RELATED QUESTIONS: *Why do we pray? Why do we talk to God? Why should we pray? Why do you have to pray?*

NOTE TO PARENTS: *Our relationship with God is to be the foundation of our whole life, and prayer is the communication element of that relationship. Therefore, prayer is the key to life the way God meant it to be. Our children need to realize how important prayer is. We wouldn't forget to eat, sleep, or dress every day, and prayer is more important to our lives than those things.*

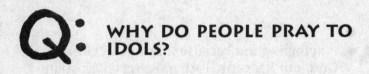

Q: WHY DO PEOPLE PRAY TO IDOLS?

6

A: Some people pray to idols because they believe that idols have power to change things. That is, they believe in a false god. They believe that their god hears and answers their prayers.

Other people pray to idols out of habit or superstition. They do not really know or believe in their idol. They just hope something will happen if they pray.

Praying to idols is wrong because idols are not really gods. They are just things. They are not alive and do not hear. They cannot answer prayers or bring good fortune. God wants us to place our trust in him and not in idols or superstitious beliefs.

KEY VERSES: *Yes, they knew God, but they wouldn't worship him as God or even give him thanks. And they began to think up foolish ideas of what God was like. The result was that their minds became dark and confused. Claiming to be wise, they became utter fools instead. And instead of worshiping the glorious, ever-living God, they worshiped idols made to look like mere people, or birds and animals and snakes. (Romans 1:21-23)*

RELATED VERSES: *Exodus 20:4; Psalm 17:6; Isaiah 2:8; 1 Corinthians 10:6-7, 14*

RELATED QUESTIONS: *What if we're praying to the wrong god and we don't know? How do we know we are praying to the right God? How come everyone needs to pray to God?*

NOTE TO PARENTS: *Making a wish when blowing out birthday candles, wishing on a star, or throwing coins into a well can be used as an example of why some people believe prayers to idols will bring them good luck. If your children wish at these times, let them know it's just for fun. If they really want something, encourage them to talk to God about it.*

Q: WHO DO WE PRAY TO—GOD OR JESUS?

DEAR HEAVENLY FATHER AND/OR JESUS...

7

A: When a person prays, it is all right to talk with God the Father, with Jesus, or with the Holy Spirit. You can find prayers to all three in the Bible. Some prayers are addressed to God the Father, some to God the Son, and some to God the Holy Spirit. That is because God is one. We have one Lord, not three. So when we pray to God the Father, we are praying to God. And when we pray to God the Son, we are praying to God. And when we pray to God the Holy Spirit, we are praying to God. We cannot mess it up by saying the wrong name.

The important thing is that the person prays to the Lord of heaven and earth, the living God. It is what is in a person's heart that counts. Beyond our words, God sees our hearts and knows our thoughts and desires.

KEY VERSE: *Dear friends, I urge you in the name of our Lord Jesus Christ to join me in my struggle by praying to God for me. Do this because of your love for me, given to you by the Holy Spirit. (Romans 15:30)*

RELATED VERSES: *Psalms 84:8; 88:1-2; Luke 11:2; Acts 4:24; Ephesians 1:17*

RELATED QUESTIONS: *Is it bad to pray to angels? Should we pray only to God?*

NOTE TO PARENTS: *Jesus taught his disciples to talk to the Father in Jesus' name. This is a good way to guide our children because most of them can understand a father-child relationship. God wants to love them, care for them, and teach them as their heavenly Father.*

Q: WHY DID JESUS PRAY?

8

A: Jesus is the God-man. That is, he is fully God and fully man, a whole human being. Because Jesus lived on earth as a man, he had human needs. It made sense for him to pray just as it makes sense for us to pray. He depended on his Father for all his needs. He also loved his Father and enjoyed being with him, so he wanted to spend time talking with him.

Jesus was also perfect. He did everything that God wanted. God told his people to pray, so Jesus obeyed his Father and prayed.

In other words, Jesus prayed for the same reasons we do—he needed God, he loved God, and he wanted to please God.

KEY VERSE: *While Jesus was here on earth, he offered prayers and pleadings, with a loud cry and tears, to the one who could deliver him out of death. And God heard his prayers because of his reverence for God. (Hebrews 5:7)*

RELATED VERSES: *Matthew 19:13; Luke 5:16; 6:12; John 17:20; Romans 8:34*

RELATED QUESTIONS: *Does Jesus pray? Does God pray?*

NOTE TO PARENTS: *God doesn't stand on the sidelines and judge our every move. He is our loving Father. He is alongside us, helping us, teaching us, caring for us. When we fall, he is right there to help us up, strengthen us, teach us, and encourage us forward.*

Q: WHEN WE'RE BAD, CAN WE STILL PRAY?

9

A: A person can pray at any time and in any need. When people do bad things or make mistakes, they need God more than at any other time. When we do something wrong, we need to talk with God about it. We need to admit that what we did was wrong, say that we're sorry, and ask him to forgive us. That is the first thing we should pray when we do something bad. Then God can help us learn so that we can do better next time. God knows we are not perfect, and he wants to help us by giving us wisdom and helping us change.

If we wait until we are good enough to pray, we will never pray.

KEY VERSES: *But the tax collector stood at a distance and dared not even lift his eyes to heaven as he prayed. Instead, he beat his chest in sorrow, saying, "O God, be merciful to me, for I am a sinner." I tell you, this sinner, not the Pharisee, returned home justified before God. For the proud will be humbled, but the humble will be honored. (Luke 18:13-14)*

RELATED VERSES: *Psalms 51:1-2; 66:18-19; Isaiah 1:15-20*

RELATED QUESTIONS: *Does everyone in the world pray? Are you only allowed to pray if you're totally good? Can animals pray? What if I injure someone? Will God still give me what I ask?*

Q: WHO IS NOT ALLOWED TO PRAY?

PRAYER CLOSET OPEN TO EVERYONE

10

A: No one is so bad that he or she is not allowed to pray. God is always willing to accept the person who comes and asks for forgiveness. God does not ban people from praying.

Some people have turned away from God so much that they never pray. They do not pray because they don't feel any need to pray and don't want to.

Are there any prayers that God does not welcome? Yes. God does not welcome the prayers of people who disobey him all the time and are happy about it. (They may even brag about their sins.) When these people pray, they do not really mean to have a relationship with God. Instead, they just go through the motions. Prayers from people like that are just empty words. The first *real* prayer that God wants to hear from them is *I have sinned. I was wrong. I am sorry. Please forgive me.*

KEY VERSE: *The Lord is far from the wicked, but he hears the prayers of the righteous. (Proverbs 15:29)*

RELATED VERSES: *Proverbs 28:9; Isaiah 1:15-16; Zechariah 13:9; 1 Timothy 2:8*

RELATED QUESTIONS: *How can you pray when you're a baby? Do people who aren't Christians ever pray? Does the devil pray? If you don't have God in your heart, should you ask him (for things)? Can sinners pray?*

Q:
WHY DO WE HAVE TO PRAY WHEN GOD ALREADY KNOWS WHAT WE ARE GOING TO PRAY?

11

A: When we pray, we talk to God about the things that we and God are doing together. God designed the universe to work a certain way, and prayer is part of his plan for how it works.

One of the most important reasons for praying is that it changes the person who is praying. When we pray, we become more like God wants us to be. *We* learn something from *God!*

Also, God wants to have a friendship with us. No one would say, "Why do we have to talk to our friends?" Talking with God just grows out of loving him and being cared for by him.

KEY VERSES: *When you pray, don't babble on and on as people of other religions do. They think their prayers are answered only by repeating their words again and again. Don't be like them, because your Father knows exactly what you need even before you ask him! (Matthew 6:7-8)*

RELATED VERSES: *Psalms 32:5-6; 139:4; Ephesians 6:18; Philippians 4:6; Colossians 4:2*

RELATED QUESTIONS: *If God knows everything, then what's the point of praying? If God knows everything we're saying and everything we're thinking, why do we have to pray at all? How does God know what we're going to say? How does God know everything? How does God know what we're thinking? Why does God know everything?*

NOTE TO PARENTS: *Help and encourage your children to say prayers that do not always involve asking for something. They can talk to God about what is going on in their lives and tell him what they are excited about. Also, encourage them to ask for needs that are intangible, such as wisdom, guidance, and help.*

Q: IF GOD IS INVISIBLE, HOW CAN WE KNOW HE IS AROUND US?

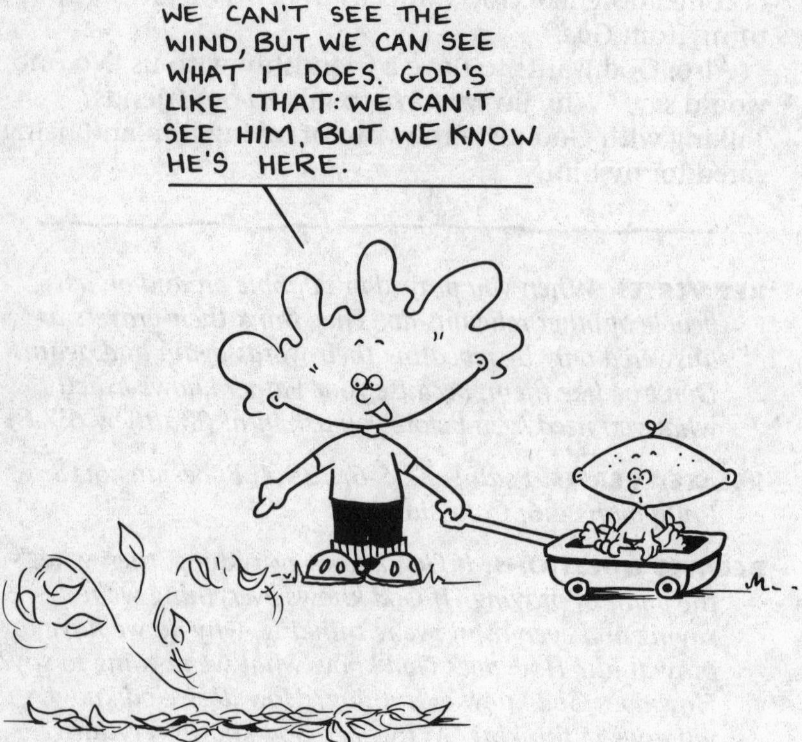

12

A: It is a little bit like believing in a country you have never been to. Other people have told you about it, you have read about it, and perhaps you have even met people from that land. All of this together tells you that the country is real. You yourself have never been there, but that does not stop you from believing it exists. You have plenty of good reasons to believe that it does.

Although we cannot see God, we know by faith that he is around us. That is, we accept that God is there because the Bible says so, because we have met God's people, and because it makes sense to us. So by faith we believe and trust that he is there even though he is invisible.

KEY VERSE: *From the time the world was created, people have seen the earth and sky and all that God made. They can clearly see his invisible qualities—his eternal power and divine nature. So they have no excuse whatsoever for not knowing God. (Romans 1:20)*

RELATED VERSES: *Psalms 23:4; 139:7-12; John 3:7-8*

RELATED QUESTIONS: *When you're praying, how can you feel God? Why is God invisible? Sometimes it's kind of hard to pray to an invisible person. If I can't see God, how can he see me? How come you can't see God? Is God invisible? Why is God invisible?*

NOTE TO PARENTS: *When your children ask why they can't see God, make sure you explain that God is invisible because he does not have a body like ours, not because he is trying to hide from us. As we get to know him better, we begin to see how he works on our behalf and how he shows his love.*

Q: HOW CAN GOD BE EVERYWHERE?

SCRATCH
SCRATCH

BIBLE

13

A: God is spirit, not just a big person. That is, God is not limited to space and time. He has no body that can only be here or there.

Also, God is *all-powerful,* not just very powerful. That is, he can do anything. He can be all places at once just by wanting to.

We human beings have physical bodies; we can be in only one place at a time. But God is not like that. He is always there to love us, to help us, and to listen to our prayers. And he wants us to know this so we will never be afraid to come to him.

KEY VERSE: *But who can really build him a worthy home? Not even the highest heavens can contain him! So who am I to consider building a Temple for him, except as a place to burn sacrifices to him? (2 Chronicles 2:6)*

RELATED VERSES: *Job 42:2-3; Psalms 103:22; 139:2-3, 7-8; Proverbs 15:3*

RELATED QUESTIONS: *How does God stay by everyone at once? Is God always watching us? How does God know what we're doing right now? How can God be within us all at one time? How does God go to three places at once?*

NOTE TO PARENTS: *The fact that God is everywhere and sees and knows everything should be a comfort to your children. He is always there to love, help, and listen. He does not merely spy on us or wait for us to mess up so he can punish us. Trying to make children behave by telling them that God is watching every move they make puts God in the wrong role.*

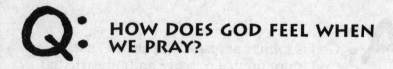

Q: HOW DOES GOD FEEL WHEN WE PRAY?

14

A: God is very happy when we pray. The Bible makes it clear that God is glad to hear from us and rejoices over us. He loves us and wants us to love him. So God is delighted when we come before him, just as a loving father is happy when his children come to him. The father welcomes his children with open arms and listens carefully to everything they say because he loves them so much.

KEY VERSE: *The Lord hates the sacrifice of the wicked, but he delights in the prayers of the upright. (Proverbs 15:8)*

RELATED VERSES: *Psalm 141:2; Isaiah 62:5; Zephaniah 3:17*

RELATED QUESTION: *Does God love the people who don't pray to Jesus?*

NOTE TO PARENTS: *This is a good opportunity to reinforce God's extravagant love for us. Take every opportunity to tell your children how much God loves and cares for them.*

Q: HOW DO WE PRAY?

NO PEEKING.

15

A: People pray in many different ways. All prayers don't have to be alike. So we should not worry about saying just the right words or holding our hands a certain way. God wants us to be ourselves and talk to him about the things that we are thinking about, concerned about, or excited about. We can talk to God in our very own words.

At the same time, we should realize that we are talking with the Creator and Ruler of everything. Even though God wants us to use our own words when we pray, he does not want us to be silly or to make a joke of prayer. We should be very respectful toward God.

KEY VERSES: *Pray like this: Our Father in heaven, may your name be honored. May your Kingdom come soon. May your will be done here on earth, just as it is in heaven. Give us our food for today, and forgive us our sins, just as we have forgiven those who have sinned against us. And don't let us yield to temptation, but deliver us from the evil one. (Matthew 6:9-13)*

RELATED VERSES: *Jeremiah 29:13; Luke 11:2-4; James 4:10; 1 Peter 4:7*

RELATED QUESTIONS: *What if you didn't know how to pray? Should we pray like Jesus when we pray? How should we pray to Jesus? What happens when we pray in a bad way?*

NOTE TO PARENTS: *Try not to reduce prayer to a set of how-to's. Prayer is about having a relationship with God. Any relationship a child has with God will be a little different from an adult's. Relax. God loves being with your children in all their different stages of growth, just as you do. Make prayer relevant by encouraging your children to be themselves.*

Q: HOW DOES GOD KNOW WHAT WE'RE SAYING IF WE'RE PRAYING IN OUR HEAD?

16

A: God knows everything, even what we keep to ourselves. He knows every thought of every person on earth. He knows what is in everyone's head. Nothing that anyone thinks or feels is hidden from God.

Praying silently means focusing our thoughts on God and talking to him in our head. He hears every silent prayer.

Of course, sometimes it is better to pray aloud, such as when we are praying with another person. And praying aloud can help us concentrate when we are praying on our own. But God hears us either way, whether we say the words or just think them.

KEY VERSES: *O Lord, you have examined my heart and know everything about me. You know when I sit down or stand up. You know my every thought when far away. (Psalm 139:1-2)*

RELATED VERSES: *Psalms 94:11; 139:23-24; Matthew 6:6-8*

RELATED QUESTIONS: *People say that God just wants you to talk to him like he's your good friend. Is this true? What kind of prayer should we pray? How does God hear you when you're not talking? How do you pray without saying anything out loud? How come people pray with their mouths closed? Why do people whisper when they pray? Is it better to pray in your heart than to pray out loud?*

NOTE TO PARENTS: *From time to time your children may ask if they can pray a certain prayer silently or to themselves. Encourage them to do so. It is a good sign that they are trusting God with things close to their heart that they may feel embarrassed to say even to you.*

Q: IS IT OK IF WE PRAY REALLY FAST OR SLOW?

THANK YOU
GOD, AMEN.

17

A: The speed of a prayer is not important. What matters is that we pray in a thoughtful manner. Sometimes we pray fast because we are excited. That is fine. But people who pray *very* fast may just be repeating a memorized prayer or saying certain words out of habit and trying to finish quickly. Whenever we pray, God is listening right then, and he does not want us to just speed through some words that we always say.

Sometimes we pray slowly because we are being thoughtful about what we want to say to God. But sometimes we pray slowly because we are letting our thoughts wander. It is always best to keep our attention on God.

Fast, medium, or slow, prayer should be a real talk with our heavenly Father.

KEY VERSES: *As you enter the house of God, keep your ears open and your mouth shut! Don't be a fool who doesn't realize that mindless offerings to God are evil. And don't make rash promises to God, for he is in heaven, and you are only here on earth. So let your words be few. (Ecclesiastes 5:1-2)*

RELATED VERSES: *1 Kings 8:54-55; Ecclesiastes 5:3, 7; Matthew 6:7; Hebrews 10:22*

RELATED QUESTIONS: *How does someone pray in sign language? Does it make a difference if you pray silently or aloud? Do you have to pray slowly so God can hear you?*

NOTE TO PARENTS: *Before praying with your children, help them think of a few things they are concerned or excited about, and encourage them to talk to God about these things. This will help make each day's prayers sincere and relevant and not just something to get done.*

Q: DOES HOW WE PRAY MATTER?

18

A: Yes. We should pray *sincerely, secretly,* and *respectfully.* To pray sincerely means to pray in plain words that say just what we mean to say. It means we do not try to use fake language or fancy words. We tell God whatever is on our mind in the words that we would normally use, because he loves us and knows us and wants to care for us.

To pray secretly means to make a habit of praying alone. (Some people call it quiet time.) It means we take time out of every day to talk to God all by ourselves. We do not limit our prayers to church, meals, or bedtime with Mom or Dad.

To pray respectfully means to treat God as God. It means we do not make light of prayer or act silly. We are talking to God, the Maker of all creation, the Lord of the universe, and the King of kings, so we show him honor and respect.

KEY VERSE: *The sacrifice you want is a broken spirit. A broken and repentant heart, O God, you will not despise. (Psalm 51:17)*

RELATED VERSES: *Proverbs 1:7; 28:9; Matthew 6:5-13; Hebrews 10:22*

RELATED QUESTIONS: *Why do some people pray in different languages? How come people pray when they're talking out loud? How come people mouth words when they pray? Do people whisper prayers because they're embarrassed?*

NOTE TO PARENTS: *If we get wrapped up in exactly how our kids must behave, position themselves, or talk when praying, they may get the idea that God expects a performance instead of a sincere expression. Give your children room to grow in the exact way they pray.*

Q: WHY DO PASTORS PRAY LONG PRAYERS?

19

A: Pastors pray long prayers because they have a lot to pray about. They are responsible for caring for a lot of people and want to pray for the concerns those people have.

Also, a lot of people ask pastors to pray for them. Many churches have a "pastor's prayer" as part of the worship service. At that time the pastor prays aloud for the needs of the people. At the same time, the people in the congregation should also pray, silently, for each need that the pastor mentions.

Keep in mind that God listens to kids just as much as to pastors. If you pray, God hears and answers your prayers the same as he does for the pastor.

KEY VERSES: *So we have continued praying for you ever since we first heard about you. We ask God to give you a complete understanding of what he wants to do in your lives, and we ask him to make you wise with spiritual wisdom. Then the way you live will always honor and please the Lord, and you will continually do good, kind things for others. All the while, you will learn to know God better and better. (Colossians 1:9-10)*

RELATED VERSES: *1 Chronicles 21:16; Acts 2:42; 6:2-4; 1 Thessalonians 1:2; 5:17; 1 Timothy 2:1-4*

RELATED QUESTIONS: *Why do some people pray very long prayers? Sometimes I want to stop praying. Should I? Is there a limit to your praying? How many words do you have to pray? Why do our pastors pray?*

NOTE TO PARENTS: *God hears and answers your child's prayers as much as he does a pastor's. Be careful not to give your children the idea that their prayers are not as effective as those of "important" people.*

Q: WHY DO PEOPLE PRAY ON THEIR KNEES?

humble   happy   tired

20

A: The Bible tells of people praying in all sorts of positions. Some stood and raised their hands. Some lay down on the ground. Some put their head between their knees. Some sat down. Some kneeled. Some stood but bowed their head and beat on their chest. We can pray in almost any position.

Some people kneel in prayer to show respect for God. It is their way of saying that they want to do things God's way. Kneeling makes them feel humble and submissive to God, which is the right attitude to have in prayer.

KEY VERSES: *He walked away, about a stone's throw, and knelt down and prayed, "Father, if you are willing, please take this cup of suffering away from me. Yet I want your will, not mine." (Luke 22:41-42)*

RELATED VERSES: *1 Kings 8:54; 2 Chronicles 6:13; Acts 20:36; James 4:10*

RELATED QUESTIONS: *Why do you kneel down or bow your head when you pray? Do you have to be in a certain position when you pray? Is it more respectful to get on your knees when you pray? Is getting on your knees a symbol of humbling yourself? Why do people pray sitting down? Why do people pray lying down? Why do we go on our knees or sit down when we pray? Is it better to pray on your knees? What is the difference between praying when you're standing or sitting?*

Q: DO WE HAVE TO FOLD OUR HANDS TO PRAY?

LESS TEMPTED | MORE TEMPTED

21

A: No. Our hands can be in any position when we pray. It is not the position of our hands that God loves but the attitude of our heart.

But most people fold their hands for a good reason. Some fold their hands to show respect and that they are bringing a request. Sometimes people fold their hands to keep them from doing anything else that might distract them from focusing on their prayer. So folding hands during prayer can be a good idea, but God does not require it. In the Bible, God's people often raised their hands to pray, as some people do today.

KEY VERSE: *So wherever you assemble, I want men to pray with holy hands lifted up to God, free from anger and controversy. (1 Timothy 2:8)*

RELATED VERSES: *Psalms 28:2; 37:7; 46:10; 141:2*

RELATED QUESTIONS: *Does it make any difference whether you fold your hands or put your hands over your head when you pray? Do you have to have your eyes closed and hands folded to pray? Why do people bow their heads when they pray? Why do most people fold their hands when they pray? Does it matter if we don't fold our hands? Why do some people stare when we raise both hands above our heads or fold our hands?*

NOTE TO PARENTS: *It is not that a particular position for your hands or body must be followed, but once a position is chosen, a reminder to stay in that position until the "amen" can really help concentration.*

Q: SHOULD WE MAKE THE SIGN OF THE CROSS WHEN WE PRAY?

22

A: Some people make the sign of the cross when they pray to show that their prayer is in "Jesus' name" (because Jesus died on the cross). It is a bit like folding hands or kneeling—God does not require it of us, but some people do it to help them pray. It reminds them that God hears their prayers because Jesus died for them.

Always remember that God cares more about our being honest and sincere than about the exact way we sit, stand, kneel, or move when we pray.

KEY VERSE: *We do this by keeping our eyes on Jesus, on whom our faith depends from start to finish. He was willing to die a shameful death on the cross because of the joy he knew would be his afterward. Now he is seated in the place of highest honor beside God's throne in heaven. (Hebrews 12:2)*

RELATED VERSE: *Galatians 6:14*

RELATED QUESTION: *Does God care how you pray as long as you're praying?*

NOTE TO PARENTS: *If you teach your children certain traditions in prayer, take the time to explain what they mean and why you feel they are important. Helping your children understand a tradition will help them get more out of it.*

Q: WHY DO WE SHUT OUR EYES WHEN WE PRAY?

THANK YOU LORD, FOR
PORK CHOPS AND MASHED
POTATOES AND THE
PUDDING AND...

23

A: We shut our eyes mainly to help us concentrate on our prayers. Whenever our eyes are open, we can see everything going on around us, and then we think about those things. We don't think so much about God or about talking to him. So people close their eyes when they pray because it helps them concentrate on what they are saying.

We can pray with our eyes open. Eyes open or shut doesn't matter to God. It's just that we need help concentrating, and closing our eyes helps us do that.

KEY VERSE: *But the tax collector stood at a distance and dared not even lift his eyes to heaven as he prayed. Instead, he beat his chest in sorrow, saying, "O God, be merciful to me, for I am a sinner." (Luke 18:13)*

RELATED VERSES: *Psalm 123:1-2; John 17:1*

RELATED QUESTIONS: *Why does my dad make me shut my eyes when I pray and then when I tell him it doesn't say in the Bible we have to, I get sent to my room? Is it best to pray when you're closing your eyes? Does it really matter whether our eyes are open or shut when we pray? Why do your parents and teachers make you close your eyes when you pray? What difference does it make if I close my eyes when I pray, or not?*

NOTE TO PARENTS: *Some young children have trouble keeping their eyes closed. Don't fret about it. Try having them put their hands over their eyes, or just have them keep their head and hands still.*

24

A: A prayer closet is a private place where a person can pray without anyone else around. It is a place where a person can get away from the busyness and noise of life. The peace and quiet helps a person spend quiet time with God, praying honestly in private without being distracted or watched by others.

A prayer closet can be a real closet where a person can shut the door, but it can also be other kinds of places. It can be a quiet spot in the house, outdoors, or somewhere else. It can be any special spot where you and God can talk. Where do you get away from everything to talk with God?

KEY VERSE: *But when you pray, go away by yourself, shut the door behind you, and pray to your Father secretly. Then your Father, who knows all secrets, will reward you. (Matthew 6:6)*

RELATED VERSES: *Matthew 14:23; Mark 1:35; Luke 5:16; 6:12*

NOTE TO PARENTS: *One of the best ways to encourage children to pray is to let them see you do it. Tell them where you like to spend time with God alone. Talk to them about your prayer times.*

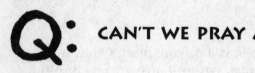

Q: CAN'T WE PRAY ANYWHERE?

THANK YOU FOR THE SUNNY DAY AT THE BEACH.

25

A: Yes, we can pray anywhere. Prayers do not have to be spoken aloud, so we can pray while we are sitting at a desk with our eyes wide open, or anywhere else. We can pray silently because God knows our thoughts. We can pray in school, on the playground, at basketball practice, in a choir concert, in church, at home, on vacation—anywhere! God is glad when we ask him for help right when and where we need it.

KEY VERSE: *Pray at all times and on every occasion in the power of the Holy Spirit. Stay alert and be persistent in your prayers for all Christians everywhere. (Ephesians 6:18)*

RELATED VERSES: *Isaiah 38:2; Matthew 6:5-6; Luke 5:16; 1 Peter 3:12*

RELATED QUESTION: *Where should we pray?*

NOTE TO PARENTS: *Our children can learn spontaneous prayer from us. Next time you are with the kids and you think of something you should pray about, ask them to join in and just do it briefly and naturally.*

Q: DO WE HAVE TO PRAY CERTAIN PRAYERS?

ORDER BY NUMBER

1. PRAYER FOR FOOD
2. PRAYER FOR HEALTH
3. PRAYER FOR FAMILY
4. PRAYER FOR SCHOOL
5. PRAYER FOR TOYS
6. DELUXE COMBO PRAYER
   (ALL OF THE ABOVE)

DRIVE-THROUGH PRAYER REQUESTS

26

A: No. We do not have to pray certain prayers, but it is OK to have certain prayers that we pray often. Written prayers can be helpful. The Lord's Prayer and the Psalms, for example, are good things to pray, and they help us think of ways to pray and things we can talk to God about. Some people memorize prayers and recite them at mealtimes or at bedtime. We just need to be careful that we really mean the words as we say them. If we say them over and over again, we may not pay attention to what we are saying.

KEY VERSE: *Give thanks to the Lord and proclaim his greatness. Let the whole world know what he has done. (1 Chronicles 16:8)*

RELATED VERSES: *Psalm 13:5-6; Luke 11:2-4*

NOTE TO PARENTS: *Children will often say things a certain way or pray certain prayers because they imagine the words themselves to have power, like magic spells. Encourage your children to pray with their own words, from the heart, and not to get stuck in a pattern of praying only certain prayers. Remind them that they are talking to their heavenly Father—someone who loves them!*

Q: WHY DID JESUS SAY WE SHOULD PRAY THE LORD'S PRAYER?

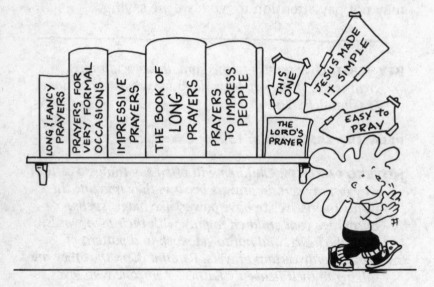

27

A: When the disciples asked Jesus to teach them how to pray, Jesus gave them the Lord's Prayer. It is a sample prayer that shows how we should pray. In other words, it is a guide and an example, not the exact words we must say every time. It shows us a good way to pray and some good topics to pray about.

For example, it tells us that we should ask God to meet our needs. It shows us that we should pray for God's will to be done in everything that happens. And it tells us to pray that we will be strong and resist temptation. It is always good to pray that way. And it is OK for us to use our own words when we do.

KEY VERSES: *Once when Jesus had been out praying, one of his disciples came to him as he finished and said, "Lord, teach us to pray, just as John taught his disciples." He said, "This is how you should pray: Father, may your name be honored. May your Kingdom come soon. Give us our food day by day. And forgive us our sins— just as we forgive those who have sinned against us. And don't let us yield to temptation." (Luke 11:1-4)*

RELATED VERSES: *Matthew 6:9-13*

RELATED QUESTIONS: *Does God want you to always say the Lord's Prayer? Why don't they change the Lord's Prayer? Why do people say the Lord's Prayer? Why do we need to learn the Lord's Prayer? We all pray in our own way.*

Q: IS IT BAD TO MEMORIZE A PRAYER AND SAY IT EVERY TIME WE PRAY?

... AND PLEASE BE WITH MOM AND DAD AND LIL...

ZZZZZ

WRRRR

28

A: It is never bad to pray a sincere and humble prayer, and memorized prayers can surely be part of that. The problem with memorized prayers is that we might get to know the prayers so well that we only say the words without thinking about them.

What matters is our attitude. Jesus wants us to say what we mean and mean what we say, not "babble on" in prayer. Our prayers should be sincere and express our true thoughts.

KEY VERSE: *When you pray, don't babble on and on as people of other religions do. They think their prayers are answered only by repeating their words again and again. (Matthew 6:7)*

RELATED VERSES: *Ecclesiastes 5:1-3*

RELATED QUESTIONS: *Why can't people pick the right words to say? Can we talk to Jesus like we talk to our friends?*

NOTE TO PARENTS: *Memorized prayers can be very inspirational and educational. Take the time to help your children understand their meaning and what they are asking. Then encourage them to add their own words on the same topic to help make the memorized prayers relevant.*

Q: DOES GOD LISTEN TO ANY PRAYER, BIG OR SMALL?

29

A: Yes, God listens to all prayers, no matter how big or small they are. In the Bible, Nehemiah prayed that he would say the right words when he talked to the king one day. Solomon prayed for wisdom. Hannah prayed for a child. Each one of these people prayed for something that mattered to him or her. It did not matter whether the prayer was big or small. They just brought their cares to God.

That is what God wants us to do. The important question is, what is on our mind? What do we care about? God will listen to any prayer if it is sincere.

KEY VERSE: *Give all your worries and cares to God, for he cares about what happens to you. (1 Peter 5:7)*

RELATED VERSES: *Nehemiah 2:4-5; Psalms 66:19; 116:1; 145:19; Proverbs 15:29*

RELATED QUESTION: *Why do you start to pray with "Dear Lord"?*

NOTE TO PARENTS: *Always encourage your children to take their concerns to God, even if those concerns seem small or simple.*

Q: WHY DO PEOPLE SAY "THEE" AND "THOU" WHEN THEY PRAY?

YEA LORD, I BESEECH THEE THAT THOU WOULDST OPEN THINE HAND AND GRANT UNTO THY SERVANT A 4×4 FULLY OPERATIONAL KIDS' JEEP WITH ALL THE ACCESSORIES.

30

A: Some people say "thee" and "thou" because they are used to it. Many years ago, the King James Version was the only English Bible. When it was written, everyone used *thee* and *thou* when they talked, so that version of the Bible has many "thees," "thous," and other words that people do not say anymore. People learned to talk to God that way because that is the way they read it in the King James Version.

Some people also feel that praying in this older style helps them show respect to God; they feel it is a more appropriate way to speak to him than to use normal language, because God is a holy and awesome God.

God wants us to talk to him in plain, everyday language. God does not care about the exact words or style of English we use as long as we say what we mean. He understands.

KEY VERSE: *Since we are receiving a Kingdom that cannot be destroyed, let us be thankful and please God by worshiping him with holy fear and awe. (Hebrews 12:28)*

RELATED VERSES: *Psalms 7:17; 47:2; 111:9; Daniel 9:4; Acts 19:17*

RELATED QUESTIONS: *If "thee" and "you" mean the same thing, why would people think God preferred them to say "thou"? How do people know God likes "thou" words? Is it all right if I say "you," or do I have to say "thee" and "thou" when I pray to God?*

NOTE TO PARENTS: *If we talk to God in plain, sincere language, our children will feel more comfortable praying than if they hear us use formal language. Using special words or tones for prayer will give them the impression that these details matter more than the content.*

Q: WHY DO WE SAY "AMEN" WHEN WE'RE DONE PRAYING?

31

A: *Amen* means "So be it" or "It is true." It is simply a way of closing a prayer. We close letters with a similar word, *sincerely. Amen* means that we have said what we mean and believe that God has heard our prayer.

To say *amen*—"So be it"—is a way of saying that we trust God to answer. It reminds us that God has everything under control.

KEY VERSE: *Blessed be the Lord, the God of Israel, from everlasting to everlasting! Let all the people say, "Amen!" Praise the Lord! (Psalm 106:48)*

RELATED VERSES: *Nehemiah 8:6; Psalm 41:13; 1 Corinthians 14:16; 2 Corinthians 1:20; Revelation 1:7*

RELATED QUESTIONS: *Do we have to say "amen" when we finish praying? Do you have to say "amen" at the end of a prayer? Why do people say "amen" while others are still praying? Does it really matter if we say "amen" at the end of our prayers? Why do some people say "amen" when I pray?*

NOTE TO PARENTS: *Be sure to explain to your children what* amen *means and that it is a declaration of their trust in God's love for them.*

Q: WHY DO WE CALL IT "SAYING GRACE"?

32

A: The word *grace* means "thanks to God." It can also be used to mean "I ask for God's favor." This is how the apostle Paul used it to close some of his letters, such as Galatians, 1 Timothy, Philemon, and others. When we pray before meals, we are thanking God for the food and asking for his blessing on that time of eating. So this prayer is called grace.

Praying before meals is a way of showing that we depend on God. It reminds us that all we have comes from God. This is an important part of prayer—thanking God for life and everything else he gives us.

KEY VERSE: *So let us come boldly to the throne of our gracious God. There we will receive his mercy, and we will find grace to help us when we need it. (Hebrews 4:16)*

RELATED VERSES: *Romans 1:7; 16:20; Revelation 22:21*

RELATED QUESTIONS: *Why do we pray before we eat? Why do you have to say grace? Why do Christians say grace? Do we have to pray before every meal? Why do we thank God for the food?*

NOTE TO PARENTS: *Thank-you prayers are important, and it is important to teach children to include them in their prayers every day. It helps them learn that God loves and cares for them and that he is the source and owner of all they have.*

Q: WHAT IS THE DIFFERENCE BETWEEN FOOD THAT WE PRAY FOR AND FOOD THAT WE HAVE NOT PRAYED FOR?

33

A: There is no difference between the two kinds of food. Praying at meals does not change the food. It changes us. We pray over the food to thank God for it and to ask his blessing on those who eat it, just the way Jesus did. We are saying, "God, we know that you have provided this food. We are thankful for it, and we ask you to use it to make us strong and healthy." We are asking God to bless the people at the meal.

Praying at meals reminds us that every bit of food we get comes from God's hand and that God provides everything we need.

KEY VERSE: *As they sat down to eat, he took a small loaf of bread, asked God's blessing on it, broke it, then gave it to them. (Luke 24:30)*

RELATED VERSES: *Matthew 14:19; 26:26; 1 Corinthians 10:31*

RELATED QUESTIONS: *When some people pray for food, they say, "Bless it to our bodies." Why? How come God blesses the food when he provided it? What happens if you forget to say grace before you eat? Can you pray when you're already eating? Should you pray even when you have a snack? Do we have to pray before breakfast? Do you have to pray at lunchtime? Are you supposed to pray before dinner? Is it OK to pray after the meal? Is it OK to pray in the middle of the meal? How much food can you eat before you stop to pray for it? What if someone's praying and someone's already eating? What if you have lunch with people who don't know God and they don't pray?*

Q: WHY DO WE HAVE TO THANK GOD AT EVERY MEAL WHEN HE ALREADY KNOWS WE'RE THANKFUL?

DITTO FROM THE PRAYER I PRAYED AT BREAKFAST.

JASON'S LUNCH

34

A: Thanking God for food is a good habit to form because it reminds us to be thankful for all that God gives us. Sometimes we think we are thankful when we really aren't. Pausing to say thank you helps us renew our thankfulness. If we just sit down and eat without thanking God every time, we can easily and quickly forget to be thankful. We can forget that our food comes from God.

It is also a nice thing to do. We say thank you to God because he is our friend and he has done something kind for us. Don't you like it when your friends say thank you to you?

KEY VERSE: *And whatever you do or say, let it be as a representative of the Lord Jesus, all the while giving thanks through him to God the Father. (Colossians 3:17)*

RELATED VERSES: *1 Chronicles 23:30; Psalm 106:1; John 6:11; 1 Corinthians 10:30; Ephesians 5:4*

RELATED QUESTIONS: *Why do we thank God for our food? Shouldn't we thank God for the food, not our parents? Why do you thank God for your food and not your parents? Why do we thank God for food if our parents prepared it?*

NOTE TO PARENTS: *Mealtime prayer with the family is a good time for your children to start learning to pray with others. Wait until they're ready, and help them out the first few times. Take turns, and encourage adding a new prayer about something current to the regular mealtime prayer.*

Q: DO WE STILL HAVE TO THANK GOD IF WE DON'T LIKE THE FOOD?

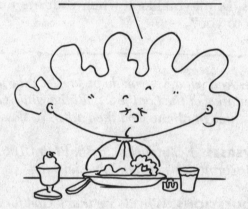

35

A: We should thank God for our food because we need food to live and God kindly gives it to us. He meets our needs even when we are not too thrilled with the way he does it.

When we pray at meals, we do not have to say that we like the food when we really do not. But it is good to say thank you to God anyway. We need to eat. Some people have very little to eat. It only makes sense to thank God that we have a meal.

KEY VERSE: *No matter what happens, always be thankful, for this is God's will for you who belong to Christ Jesus. (1 Thessalonians 5:18)*

RELATED VERSES: *Romans 1:21; 1 Corinthians 10:30-31; Ephesians 5:4, 20; 1 Timothy 4:4-5*

RELATED QUESTIONS: *What if you have to eat something you don't like and you hide it? What about throwing your food in the garbage and someone else sees it? What if you don't like the food so you don't thank God? What if you thank God and then throw the food away?*

Q: WHY DO WE PRAY BEFORE WE GO TO BED?

36

A: Because nighttime is a good time to pray. We can think about the day we had. We can thank God for all that he did and tell him about our problems and struggles. Also, we can pray for protection. We can ask God for a good night's sleep and for good dreams and to keep us from nightmares. Praying before going to bed is a good habit to form and keep. But not all people pray before going to bed. We can pray anytime.

KEY VERSE: *I will lie down in peace and sleep, for you alone, O Lord, will keep me safe. (Psalm 4:8)*

RELATED VERSES: *Psalms 42:8; 55:16-17; 119:62; 141:2*

RELATED QUESTIONS: *Why do people pray at night instead of in the daytime? Doesn't God sleep? Is it wrong to go to sleep without praying just because you don't know what to pray about? Why would you pray only at night?*

NOTE TO PARENTS: *Nighttime is a good time to teach your children to pray. It gives you an opportunity to set aside a regular, special, quiet-time of prayer without a lot of distractions. It lets you model how to pray and what kinds of concerns to bring to God. And it lets you review how God has blessed you as a family that day.*

Q: WHY DO WE HAVE TO PRAY WHEN WE DON'T WANT TO?

37

A: Eating foods that are good for us, brushing our teeth, getting up when the alarm goes off, working hard in school, practicing the piano, and cleaning up our messes are all good. We are glad we did them after they are done, but often we do them only because they need to be done, not because they are fun.

God tells us to pray because it draws us closer to God. It changes us. It helps us understand God's will better. It helps us give our worries to God. So we should pray even when we do not feel like it.

If we wait until we feel like praying, we may never do it. This is true of all good activities, not just prayer. We have to work at things that are good and important. But the rewards are always worth it.

KEY VERSE: *No discipline is enjoyable while it is happening— it is painful! But afterward there will be a quiet harvest of right living for those who are trained in this way. (Hebrews 12:11)*

RELATED VERSES: *Luke 22:46; Romans 12:12; Colossians 4:2; 1 Peter 4:7*

RELATED QUESTIONS: *What if you don't like to pray? Why should you pray if you're angry? Should you pray when you're scared? Should you pray when you have a bad dream? Why do people think God won't hear you when you're angry? What if your brother's baby-sitting you and doesn't want to pray?*

NOTE TO PARENTS: *It is important to make learning fun. But children need to understand that we pray not because it is fun but because it is vital to life. Our relationship with God is life's foundation, and prayer is the key to that relationship.*

Q: WHY DO WE HAVE TO GIVE THANKS FOR THINGS WE DON'T LIKE?

38

A: God tells us to thank him *in* all things, not *for* all things. That means that when something bad happens, we should thank God for being there with us through those bad times. This helps us remember that God is in control and that he still loves us and has a plan for us, no matter what happens.

We do not have to thank God for bad events. If something bad happens, it is bad. God does not ask us to be glad for that. Maybe a pet or a relative died. That is a bad thing, and it is OK to cry about it.

But God also tells us to be grateful for him and his plan. Some of the things we do not like are actually good for us. Maybe it is good even if we do not like it. Or maybe God has a plan that we cannot see. We need to trust in God's goodness; that is why we thank him in all things.

KEY VERSE: *Whatever you do or say, let it be as a representative of the Lord Jesus, all the while giving thanks through him to God the Father. (Colossians 3:17)*

RELATED VERSES: *Psalms 69:30; 100:4; Ephesians 5:4, 20*

RELATED QUESTIONS: *Why do you have to thank God for things that you don't want? Why do we thank God? Does God always want us to be happy with what he does? Even if we get hurt bad, do we thank God for it? I think that thanking and worshiping God is the best part of prayer, right? Is it wrong to not be thankful when God gives us something we don't want? Should you thank God for stuff?*

Q: WHY SHOULD WE GO TO GOD FOR HELP?

A: We should ask God for help because we need him. Asking why we should go to God for help is like asking "Why should I go to the gas station for gas?" God is the one who gives us life, the one who makes us able to walk, talk, and move; he is the one who gives us knowledge and the one who gives us all we need. In a sense, he is the *only* one who can help us. That is why we should go to God for help.

KEY VERSE: *In my distress I prayed to the Lord, and the Lord answered me and rescued me. (Psalm 118:5)*

RELATED VERSES: *Psalms 17:6; 118:7-9; 144:2; Hebrews 13:6*

RELATED QUESTIONS: *If someone's in trouble and not praying, should you pray for them? Do we pray when we need to?*

NOTE TO PARENTS: *The world does not teach children to recognize God as their source of help. They will need to learn it from you. Point your children to God in prayer as the first stop on the way to getting help and finding answers.*

Q: WHY DO PEOPLE WAIT UNTIL THE LAST MINUTE TO PRAY?

40

A: Some people wait till the last minute to pray because they forget or because they do not think they need God's help. They rely on themselves so much that they think they can do almost anything on their own. Or they may have forgotten about God. Then, when things get worse, they cry out to God for help as a last resort.

Instead of doing those things, we should remember that we need God's help all the time. We should talk with him *first* in every situation we face.

Of course, we should not wait until we have a huge problem to pray. We should talk with God about everything. We should praise the Lord every day because it reminds us that he is there, he loves us, and he is in charge of everything that happens. That helps us avoid a lot of problems in the first place.

KEY VERSE: *Praise the Lord, I tell myself, and never forget the good things he does for me. (Psalm 103:2)*

RELATED VERSES: *Deuteronomy 6:12; Psalms 107:12-13, 18-19, 25-28; 118:8-9; 119:93; Colossians 4:2; 2 Peter 3:5*

RELATED QUESTION: *Why do people only pray when they have a problem?*

NOTE TO PARENTS: *People begin to grow in prayer when they turn to God during times of calm. Pray together with your children even when you have everything you need. This will help them mature in their prayer habits.*

Q: WHAT HAPPENS IF WE DON'T PRAY AT ALL?

41

A: People who do not pray at all grow distant from God, like friends who grow apart because they never talk to each other. Friends keep their friendship close by talking with each other. People who never talk to each other become almost like strangers. People who do not pray miss out on getting to know God better.

Also, people who do not pray miss out on God's help. It is the people who call out to God who get to see God work most. They see him change things and people in awesome ways. They learn things that they could not have learned on their own. People who do not pray cut themselves off from this special part of God's plan.

We need to stay close to God, and we need his power. Prayer meets those needs.

KEY VERSE: *[Jesus said,] "And so I tell you, keep on asking, and you will be given what you ask for. Keep on looking, and you will find. Keep on knocking, and the door will be opened." (Luke 11:9)*

RELATED VERSES: *1 Samuel 12:23; Psalms 14:4-5; 120:1; Matthew 26:41; James 5:16*

RELATED QUESTIONS: *How can people have so many prayers? How would we know to pray for someone if we didn't know they needed it? Should you always pray to God if you have any questions? Why should we pray when we feel we should?*

NOTE TO PARENTS: *We need to be very clear with our children on this issue. God will not force himself into our lives. It is not true that a person can walk with God without prayer. Prayer is God's plan and program for having a relationship with him.*

Q: WHAT HAPPENS IF WE'RE INTERRUPTED WHEN WE'RE PRAYING?

DOES GOD HAVE CALL ALERT?

42

A: It is just like a conversation with somebody else—we stop until we can pick up where we left off later. Of course, if we keep getting interrupted in our prayers, we should try to find a place and time where we can pray without any distractions. But it is OK to start praying again if we get interrupted in the middle of a prayer.

KEY VERSE: *Jesus often withdrew to the wilderness for prayer. (Luke 5:16)*

RELATED VERSES: *Mark 1:35; Acts 10:9; 1 Peter 4:7*

RELATED QUESTIONS: *What about being distracted while you're praying?*

Q: WHAT DOES "PRAYING CONTINUALLY" MEAN?

SEEING EYE HEDGEHOG

43

A: When the Bible talks about praying continually, it means always being ready to pray. It means checking in with God throughout the day. It means that our *first* response when something happens is to pray. When something bad happens, we ask for help. When something good happens, we thank God. When we do not know what to do, we ask God to give us wisdom. It means talking to him as a friend and as a loving Father who is always around.

When you think about it, it makes perfect sense. God *is* our Friend and loving Father who is always around!

KEY VERSE: *Keep on praying. (1 Thessalonians 5:17)*

RELATED VERSES: *Ephesians 6:18; 2 Timothy 1:3*

RELATED QUESTIONS: *How many times should you pray a day? How often should we pray? Why don't people pray all the time? When it says "pray continually," does it mean you have to pray every hour? Why do we have to pray continually? Should we always pray? Will God still love us?*

NOTE TO PARENTS: *Our children need to know that we pray because of our relationship with God. We pray to get to know him better and to develop our relationship with him. That is prayer's purpose. Do not leave your children with the impression that prayer is always a dry time of merely covering the day's issues.*

Q: DOES PRAYING A LOT MAKE A PERSON BETTER?

44

A: Yes. Praying a lot makes a person better because it draws that person closer to God. Prayer makes a person more sensitive to God's will, to others, and to what is important. Praying gets the focus off one's self and onto God. When we spend time with God, we become more like him, just the way we become more like the friends we hang around with.

We just need to be careful not to compare ourselves with others. We need to concentrate on praying more, not on praying more than someone else we know.

KEY VERSE: *Devote yourselves to prayer with an alert mind and a thankful heart. (Colossians 4:2)*

RELATED VERSES: *Psalm 77:11-12; Acts 2:42; 1 Thessalonians 3:10; James 5:16; 1 Peter 3:12*

RELATED QUESTIONS: *Am I supposed to pray every day? Why do we have to pray every day? Do we need to pray more than once every day? Can I just pray grace every day?*

NOTE TO PARENTS: *Longer prayers come from sincere conversation with God, not from a concern with longer prayers. Let your children grow in prayer as a result of their growing relationship with God. Do not focus on how many minutes they spend praying each day.*

Q: CAN WE PRAY ANYTIME WE WANT?

45

A: Yes, we can pray to God anytime we want. God does not mind if we pray between meals, after bedtime prayer (when we can't sleep), or in school. Because of Christ, the door to God is always open. We can always go to him.

Of course, we need to respect others. We should not start praying out loud in the middle of a conversation with our friends. But if we are in a group, we can still take a moment to pray silently if we need to.

KEY VERSE: *Pray at all times and on every occasion in the power of the Holy Spirit. Stay alert and be persistent in your prayers for all Christians everywhere. (Ephesians 6:18)*

RELATED VERSES: *Psalm 86:3; Colossians 4:2*

RELATED QUESTIONS: *Why are there special times to pray? What is the best time to pray? What are the special times that it's good to pray? Should you pray on holidays? Do people pray every day and every night? How come you have to pray every day? What if you don't pray for a whole year? When should we pray?*

NOTE TO PARENTS: *Keep affirming how pleased God is with your children when they pray and how much he loves to talk to them. We want to spend time with the people we love, and so does God. He is pleased when his children come to him in prayer.*

Q: WHAT DO WE NEED TO PRAY FOR?

46

A: We need to pray for three things: (1) our needs, (2) the needs of others, and (3) God's will to be done. Many of the requests we bring to God will be one of these kinds of prayers.

For example, we need food, clothing, and shelter. So do other people. We also need forgiveness, and help in resisting temptation, doing good, and becoming what God wants us to be.

We also need to pray for God's will to be done on earth. Jesus taught us to pray, "May your will be done here on earth, just as it is in heaven" (Matthew 6:10). This is also one reason the Bible tells us to pray for leaders. We can affect events in the world by praying this way.

We do not have to limit our prayers to needs. We can praise God and tell him how wonderful he is. God is our friend. He wants to hear from us.

KEY VERSES: *He said, "This is how you should pray: Father, may your name be honored. May your Kingdom come soon. Give us our food day by day. And forgive us our sins—just as we forgive those who have sinned against us. And don't let us yield to temptation." (Luke 11:2-4)*

RELATED VERSES: *Luke 11:9-10; John 16:23-24; Philippians 4:6; 1 Timothy 2:1-4*

RELATED QUESTIONS: *Does God sometimes tell us what to pray for? Why do we have to pray for things? Do you have to ask God for stuff?*

NOTE TO PARENTS: *You can introduce your children to different prayer needs one at a time. When they get a handle on one, you can move them on to the next. That way they have time to learn each one well.*

Q: ARE THERE SOME THINGS THAT WE SHOULDN'T PRAY ABOUT?

JASON'S IMAGINATION

ZAPPED BROCCOLI PATCH

47

A: If something is important to us, we should feel free to pray about it. God does not laugh at people when they pray. He does not have a list of topics that people should not pray about.

Prayer is one of the main ways God changes people for the better. If there is something wrong with the way we are praying, God will reveal it to us in a kind way. In fact, our prayer will draw us closer to God, and he will use our relationship with him to help us change. Of course, prayer should be sincere, not silly or selfish. But God will not make fun of us for talking to him about this or that topic. He will always listen to what we have to say.

It would not make sense to ask God to do something that is wrong or bad, because God never sins. But we can talk to God about anything that concerns us.

KEY VERSE: *Let us come boldly to the throne of our gracious God. There we will receive his mercy, and we will find grace to help us when we need it. (Hebrews 4:16)*

RELATED VERSES: *Matthew 7:7-11; John 14:13-14*

RELATED QUESTIONS: *Why can't we pray for other stuff besides good health and protection? Does God care what we pray about? Can you pray it would rain gold? Can you pray for animals to talk? If you are captive with the police, are you allowed to pray that you can break free?*

NOTE TO PARENTS: *Concentrate on teaching your children to turn to God in prayer as a way of life, not on restricting their prayers to a certain type. It is much more important that they develop the habit of prayer than that they "get it perfect" at a young age.*

Q: CAN WE TELL GOD EVERYTHING WE WANT TO?

AND AFTER LUNCH,
I WENT BACK TO CLASS.
AND THEN....

48

A: Yes, we can talk to God about any joy, sorrow, need, feeling, worry, doubt, or fear that is on our mind. It is important to be honest with God and say what we are thinking.

But whenever we are angry or upset, we should also try to remember that God is on our side. Job did this when he was hurt and confused. He told God how he felt, but he did not accuse God of doing something wrong just because he was so upset. He knew God was good and loved him, so Job did not take out his anger on God. David's psalms are this way too; Psalm 22 is a good example. If we are hurt or angry, we should tell God, but we should also say that we know he is good. We can also ask him to help us understand and trust him. We should not accuse God of evil or of doing bad things.

KEY VERSES: *Don't worry about anything; instead, pray about everything. Tell God what you need, and thank him for all he has done. If you do this, you will experience God's peace, which is far more wonderful than the human mind can understand. His peace will guard your hearts and minds as you live in Christ Jesus. (Philippians 4:6-7)*

RELATED VERSES: *Job 1:20-22; 2:9-10; Psalms 22:16-24; 139:23-24; 1 Timothy 4:4-5*

RELATED QUESTIONS: *Can we pray to ask God how old he is? If you pray, how many awards will you get in heaven? Is it bad to not pray for some things you already know about?*

NOTE TO PARENTS: *Help your children talk openly with God, just like they do with people they trust when they feel deeply about something. But also encourage them to be ready to learn and change.*

Q: DOES GOD WANT US TO PRAY FOR OUR FRIENDS?

49

A: God definitely wants us to pray for our friends. John 17 tells about Jesus praying for his disciples. He prayed that they would be filled with joy, made holy, unified, and protected from the evil one. Jesus thought that it was important to pray for his friends in this way.

We can also pray for our friends' problems, their attitude, that they will come to know Jesus, and that they learn to be better friends. In fact, this is one way we keep them as friends. Whatever our friends need, we can pray for them, and God welcomes such prayers.

KEY VERSE: *I urge you, first of all, to pray for all people. As you make your requests, plead for God's mercy upon them, and give thanks. (1 Timothy 2:1)*

RELATED VERSES: *Matthew 5:43-48; John 17:6-26*

RELATED QUESTIONS: *Can you pray for friends? Can we pray for kindness and love? Can you pray for your friends not to get in trouble? Can you pray for kids that don't play with you?*

NOTE TO PARENTS: *Guide your children in praying for a friend each night.*

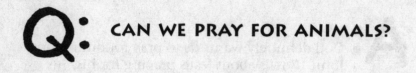

Q: CAN WE PRAY FOR ANIMALS?

A: We can pray about anything that is important to us, and that includes animals. God wants us to talk with him about the things that matter to us. He is our friend, and he cares about us. Also, God created the animals, and he loves them. So if an animal or a pet is important to us, we should feel free to pray for it. Certainly farmers should pray for their animals.

KEY VERSE: *The godly are concerned for the welfare of their animals. (Proverbs 12:10)*

RELATED VERSES: *Psalm 104:10-23; Matthew 6:26; Luke 12:24*

RELATED QUESTIONS: *Can we pray for pets? Can you pray your pets would listen to you?*

Q: DO WE HAVE TO PRAY FOR PEOPLE WE HAVEN'T MET BEFORE?

...AND BLESS A&B ADAMS

AND BLESS ANNE ADAMS

AND BLESS ARNE ADAMS...

51

A: We do not have to meet people in order to pray for them. For example, the Bible tells us to pray for government leaders. Surely we have not met all the leaders of the country, but we should pray for them anyway. We should also pray for missionaries we hear or know about, even if we have never met them. So, yes, we should pray for some of the people we have never met before.

Remember that prayer can be an adventure. We can affect decisions of the president or mayor by praying for that person. Try not to look at it as a duty or a job but as a privilege. It is kind of like helping run the country.

KEY VERSES: *Pray this way for kings and all others who are in authority, so that we can live in peace and quietness, in godliness and dignity. This is good and pleases God our Savior, for he wants everyone to be saved and to understand the truth. (1 Timothy 2:2-4)*

RELATED VERSES: *Romans 8:26-27; 15:30; Ephesians 6:18; 1 Timothy 2:1*

RELATED QUESTIONS: *Can you pray for people in other places in the world? Can we pray that God would give us enough food to give to the poor? Would God want me to pray for people that have no home? Why do we pray for other people? Can you pray for other people?*

NOTE TO PARENTS: *From time to time, lead your children in praying for people they know; then, guide them to include someone they don't know. God will help them learn to pray beyond their own experience. After all, prayer is a dialogue with God, and he will teach them as they practice and get to know him better.*

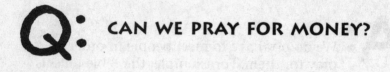

Q: CAN WE PRAY FOR MONEY?

52

A: Most certainly. We need money to survive, and God wants us to rely on him to meet our needs. So it is wise and good to pray for money and for the means to earn it.

One of the best ways to pray for money is to ask God to help us earn or work for the money we need. God may answer a prayer for money by providing a job or a gift. Or he may teach us to get by with less. When we pray for money, we should be willing to accept whatever answer God gives.

We should ask God to show us how we can use what we have more wisely. If we make better use of what we earn, we may not need any more. Sometimes God provides for us by making us better money managers.

We need to heed one caution: God says that we may not get what we ask for if we only want to spend it on our own pleasures. So when we ask God for money, we should think about how we can give some to the church and share some with others.

KEY VERSES: *You parents—if your children ask for a loaf of bread, do you give them a stone instead? Or if they ask for a fish, do you give them a snake? Of course not! If you sinful people know how to give good gifts to your children, how much more will your heavenly Father give good gifts to those who ask him. (Matthew 7:9-11)*

RELATED VERSES: *Proverbs 30:8; Matthew 6:11*

RELATED QUESTIONS: *Can we pray for things we want? Is it OK to pray for lots and lots of things? Is it OK to pray for all there is? Instead of praying for specific things, why don't you just pray for a good day and thank God for everything he did for us?*

Q: CAN WE ASK GOD TO GIVE US THINGS LIKE TOYS?

53

A: It is all right to ask God for fun things such as toys. We can talk with God about anything. But praying for something does not mean that we will get it. God knows if something is good or bad for us. He may not give us something because it is not good for us.

The Bible warns us that we should not ask God for things if we want them only for selfish reasons. Solomon knew this. God promised to give Solomon whatever he asked for. Solomon decided to ask for wisdom. God was very pleased with this. He said Solomon made the right choice because he did not ask for great wealth or power. Then God rewarded him by making him rich and powerful.

Ask for things that help others. God wants us to trust him to meet our needs.

KEY VERSES: *God said to Solomon, "Because your greatest desire is to help your people, and you did not ask for personal wealth and honor or the death of your enemies or even a long life, but rather you asked for wisdom and knowledge to properly govern my people, I will certainly give you the wisdom and knowledge you requested. And I will also give you riches, wealth, and honor such as no other king has ever had before you or will ever have again!" (2 Chronicles 1:11-12)*

RELATED VERSES: *James 4:1-3*

RELATED QUESTIONS: *Is it OK to ask for something? Does God want you to pray for the toy you wanted?*

NOTE TO PARENTS: *Help your children look to God, not things, as the source of happiness. Whenever they want to pray for toys or other fun things, guide them to ask God to do what he thinks best. This is part of teaching them to trust God to rule in their lives.*

Q: IS IT OK TO PRAY TO GET SOMETHING THAT OUR FRIENDS HAVE?

54

A: It is good to tell God what is on our mind, but it is not good to think that we need to have certain things to be happy. Having things does not make us happy. God knows this. So we should not think that if we suddenly had a new toy or piece of clothing we would be happy forever. Knowing God and obeying him is what makes us happy.

Craving what others have is called envy. God tells us not to envy because people who envy are never satisfied; they never think they have enough, even after they get all that they want. Instead of envying, God tells us to be content with what we have.

But we should still tell God how we feel. When a friend has something that we would like, we should talk with God about it, especially if it is something that we need. Then we should trust that God will give us what is best for us.

KEY VERSE: *Do not covet your neighbor's house. Do not covet your neighbor's wife, male or female servant, ox or donkey, or anything else your neighbor owns. (Exodus 20:17)*

RELATED VERSES: *1 Samuel 8:5-20; James 4:1-3*

RELATED QUESTIONS: *Can you ask for your friends' stuff? Is it wrong to ask God to give other people candy? Is it OK to pray for more of what you already have?*

NOTE TO PARENTS: *Make sure your children know about advertising and how it works. If they can learn to recognize the hard sell, they will be more prepared to handle it correctly.*

Q: IS IT BAD TO ASK GOD FOR SOMETHING WE DON'T REALLY NEED?

THANK YOU, GOD, FOR BLESSING MY <u>VEGETABLE GARDEN</u>.

VEGETABLES

55

A: It is not the *best* way to pray, but it is not bad. God invites us to come to him with our needs and concerns. He invites us to tell him how we feel. He promises to meet our needs, to care about our cares, and to work out his good plan in our lives.

That means we should ask him to meet our true needs and talk to him about our problems. It does not mean we should treat God like Santa Claus and always be asking for a long list of things that we want only for ourselves.

Sometimes we ask God for things that we *think* we need, but really we do not need them at all. It is OK to tell God we wish we had this or that thing. Whenever we pray, we should be honest and tell God our real feelings. But we should accept his answers and be content with what he gives us.

KEY VERSES: *I know how to live on almost nothing or with everything. I have learned the secret of living in every situation, whether it is with a full stomach or empty, with plenty or little. For I can do everything with the help of Christ who gives me the strength I need. (Philippians 4:12-13)*

RELATED VERSES: *Matthew 6:31-33; 7:11; Philippians 4:19*

RELATED QUESTIONS: *Can we pray for dirt bikes? Can we pray for new clothes? Can we pray for a rocket? Can we pray for a new car? Will God buy Dad a new Jeep?*

NOTE TO PARENTS: *Listen to your children's heart when they ask a question like this. Some children need encouragement to ask God for anything, and others come to prayer time with a long list. Encourage a balance, and, most important, teach kids to trust in God.*

Q: IF WE PRAYED TO FIND SOMETHING WE LOST, WOULD WE REALLY FIND IT?

JASON'S IMAGINATION

LITTLE BO PEEP
HAS LOST HER SHEEP
AND DOESN'T KNOW
WHERE TO FIND THEM,
SHE PRAYED ON HER OWN
THAT THEY WOULD COME HOME
DRAGGING THEIR TAILS
BEHIND THEM.

56

A: If it was part of God's plan for us, yes. No job is too small for God. It is good to pray for what matters to us, even something small that is lost. God may help us find it right away, or he may help us remember where we put it. He also might have us retrace our steps to find it so we will be more careful next time.

But prayer does not substitute for being careful. We should not be careless and think, "Oh, well, if I lose it, I can just ask God to find it for me." That would be using prayer the wrong way.

KEY VERSES: *As one of them was chopping, his ax head fell into the river. "Ah, my lord!" he cried. "It was a borrowed ax!" "Where did it fall?" the man of God asked. When he showed him the place, Elisha cut a stick and threw it into the water. Then the ax head rose to the surface and floated. (2 Kings 6:5-6)*

RELATED VERSES: *Psalm 139:1-2; Matthew 10:29-31; Luke 15:8*

RELATED QUESTIONS: *How does God help you find things when you lose them? When you've lost a little key, can you pray to find it? If someone stole your car, can you pray that you'll get it back?*

NOTE TO PARENTS: *Let your children hear you pray aloud, in both small matters and big ones. Also talk with them about God's answers. This will help them see how God works in your life and, therefore, in theirs.*

WHAT IF KIDS ARE MEAN TO US AND IT'S HARD FOR US TO PRAY FOR THEM?

57

A: It is not always easy to pray. But praying for kids who are mean to us is one of the best things we can do to help them. We can pray that God will help those who are mean to stop being mean. We can also pray that God will help us to be kind and loving to them so they will learn about God's love through our example. Maybe if they see God's love in us, they will come to know Jesus.

We should let God judge others. In other words, we should not pray for God to punish someone, even our enemies. Instead, we should pray that people will trust in Jesus and that they will develop a love for God. If they love God, they will stop being mean.

KEY VERSES: *[Jesus said,] "But if you are willing to listen, I say, love your enemies. Do good to those who hate you. Pray for the happiness of those who curse you. Pray for those who hurt you." (Luke 6:27-28)*

RELATED VERSES: *Matthew 5:43-48; 1 Timothy 2:8*

RELATED QUESTIONS: *What if you don't want to pray for someone? Why do we have to pray for people who are mean to us? What if people beat you up? Do you still have to pray for them? Do we have to pray for people who hate us? Does God really expect you to pray for good things to happen to bad kids, and meanwhile they still hate you? What do you do if you don't want to love and pray for your enemies? Should you pray for others even though you don't like them? Why would Jesus say to pray for our enemies who do mean things to us, if he wants us to love ourselves?*

Q: WHY DO WE PRAY FOR OUR ENEMIES?

58

A: The main reason to pray for our enemies is because God tells us to. In fact, he tells us to *love* our enemies. Praying for our enemies and loving them is God's way.

Another reason is that all people, especially bad people, need prayer. There is no better way to change them. If we want bad people to stop being bad, we need to ask God to do it. We need to pray for them so that they will change.

Jesus prayed for his enemies. He prayed for the religious leaders who wanted him to die, and he prayed for us. He did that because he loved us, even while we were God's enemies.

KEY VERSES: *But I say, love your enemies! Pray for those who persecute you! In that way, you will be acting as true children of your Father in heaven. For he gives his sunlight to both the evil and the good, and he sends rain on the just and on the unjust, too. (Matthew 5:44-45)*

RELATED VERSES: *Psalm 109:4-5; Luke 6:27-28; Romans 12:14, 19-20*

RELATED QUESTIONS: *Even if enemies kill someone you like, do you have to pray for them? Why can't we ask God to punish our enemies? Why should we pray for our enemies? If we pray for them, they'll pick on us more. Is it wrong to not pray for people you hate? If we pray for someone everyone hates, what should we do when they start hating us? Why do you have to love your enemies? Does God want us to pray for evil people?*

Q: CAN WE ASK GOD TO HELP US PASS A TEST?

59

A: We can ask God for help on a test because we can talk with God about anything. But God expects us to do our best at whatever we do. We go to school and work as part of his plan to grow us into adults. It is true that we rely on God for strength, wisdom, and life. But that is not the same as asking God to live our lives for us.

We should do our duty as students. We should study for tests and do what the teacher says. Then we should pray and ask God to give us a clear mind to take the test as well as we can, to help us relax, and to remember what we have studied.

God is merciful, and he does help us. But it helps to study for the test more than to pray for God to rescue us from a lack of studying. We can ask God to help us study.

KEY VERSES: *Work hard and cheerfully at whatever you do, as though you were working for the Lord rather than for people. Remember that the Lord will give you an inheritance as your reward, and the Master you are serving is Christ. (Colossians 3:23-24)*

RELATED VERSES: *Psalms 34:15; 55:16; Ephesians 6:18; Philippians 4:6-7; 2 Timothy 2:15*

RELATED QUESTIONS: *Could you pray for help on memorizing your verse? If we studied hard on a test, do we still have to ask God to help us to pass the test? Will God help me pass my test if I didn't study? Can you pray for the memory and study yourself? Can we pray for anything? Even good math marks? Is it wrong to not study for a test and ask for God's help?*

Q: WHEN WE'RE SAD, CAN WE PRAY THAT SOMEONE WILL COME PLAY WITH US?

DEAR LORD, PLEASE SEND A FRIEND TO PLAY WITH ME.

60

A: Yes. God cares for us, he wants us to have good friends, and he wants to comfort us when we are sad. Those are the three main reasons that it is OK to ask God to send someone to play with us when we are sad. We can talk with God about anything. It is especially important to be honest and tell him how we are feeling.

We can also pray that we can be a friend and a comfort to someone else. Maybe someone nearby is feeling lonely and needs a friend. Sometimes the best way to get a friend is to be a friend.

KEY VERSE: *Please keep a guest room ready for me, for I am hoping that God will answer your prayers and let me return to you soon. (Philemon 1:22)*

RELATED VERSE: *Hebrews 13:19*

RELATED QUESTIONS: *Is it selfish to only pray for yourself? Is it selfish to pray to be rich? Can you ask for stuff for free? When I'm lost, can I pray?*

Q: WHY DO WE PRAY TO GOD TO HELP US NOT BE BAD?

DEAR GOD, MORE THAN EVER IT IS IMPORTANT IF YOU COULD HELP ME BE GOOD.

61

A: Because we all sin. It is natural for us to do bad things. So we need God's help to do good things instead of bad. God can help us, and he wants to. In fact, God is the only one who has the power to help us overcome temptation.

When the disciples asked Jesus how to pray, he gave them what we call the Lord's Prayer. In that prayer he taught them to pray, "Don't let us yield to temptation, but deliver us from the evil one." When we pray a prayer like that, we ask God to help us not be bad.

KEY VERSE: *And don't let us yield to temptation, but deliver us from the evil one. (Matthew 6:13)*

RELATED VERSES: *Psalms 51:3; 139:23-24; 2 Corinthians 13:7, 9; Ephesians 6:19*

RELATED QUESTIONS: *Is it wrong to not pray for something that needs prayer? If we do something bad, can we pray about it?*

Q: WHY DO WE ASK JESUS INTO OUR HEART?

62

A: When we say "heart," we mean the part of us that decides everything. So when someone says that we ought to ask Jesus into our heart, the person means that we should ask Jesus to be the true master of our lives. It also means that we ask him to be our Savior, to forgive our sins, and to take care of us. That is how a person becomes a Christian. When we do this, the Holy Spirit really does come and live inside us. Then we have him with us all the time.

KEY VERSE: *I pray that Christ will be more and more at home in your hearts as you trust in him. May your roots go down deep into the soil of God's marvelous love. (Ephesians 3:17)*

RELATED VERSES: *John 16:5-7; Acts 15:8-9; 16:14; 28:26-27; Romans 5:5; 10:8-10; 2 Corinthians 3:3; Galatians 4:6-7; Revelation 3:20*

RELATED QUESTIONS: *Is Jesus knocking on your heart to let him in? How do people become Christians? Should I ask God to forgive me for my sins in general, or say each sin I have done and ask him to forgive me? Can Satan change your heart back to a black heart? Can God keep it white?*

NOTE TO PARENTS: *Whenever a question like this comes up, be prepared to talk about your children's own decision to accept Jesus. Be ready and willing to invite them to pray to receive Christ if they have never done so before.*

Q: DO WE HAVE TO PRAY TO BE FORGIVEN?

63

A: Whenever we ask God to forgive us, he forgives us. That is what the word *confession* means. It means that we tell God what we have done, agree with him that it is wrong, and ask him to forgive us. Because only God can forgive sins, we need to confess them to him in order to be truly forgiven. And we have his promise that he will always forgive if we come to him truly sorry for what we have done.

KEY VERSE: *If we confess our sins to him, he is faithful and just to forgive us and to cleanse us from every wrong. (1 John 1:9)*

RELATED VERSES: *Psalms 25:11; 32:1-6; 51:1-19; Matthew 6:12, 14-15; Mark 11:25*

RELATED QUESTIONS: *If you don't pray, do you still go to heaven? If you pray to God, will he give you better permission to go to heaven? Why did Jesus die?*

NOTE TO PARENTS: *There is no better way to teach children about confession than to show them how it is done. Always be willing to seek out forgiveness if appropriate, and let your children hear you confess sins to God.*

Q: CAN GOD HELP US PRAY?

64

A: Yes. Many times we want to talk with God but just don't know what to say or how to put our feelings into words. The Holy Spirit can help us think of the right words and say them. But even if we still don't know what to say, God knows what we are feeling and thinking. He knows that we sincerely want to talk with him, and he understands what we *would* say if we could.

The best way to pray is just to pray. That is, we should not wait until we think we have all the right words. We should just speak to God from the heart as best we can. He will understand what we mean even if we get the words messed up.

KEY VERSES: *The Holy Spirit helps us in our distress. For we don't even know what we should pray for, nor how we should pray. But the Holy Spirit prays for us with groanings that cannot be expressed in words. And the Father who knows all hearts knows what the Spirit is saying, for the Spirit pleads for us believers in harmony with God's own will. (Romans 8:26-27)*

RELATED VERSES: *Hebrews 7:25; 1 Peter 5:7*

RELATED QUESTIONS: *Why does the Holy Spirit pray for us? Does Jesus help you pray? How does God pray with us when we're praying? How would we know to pray for someone if we didn't know they needed it?*

NOTE TO PARENTS: *Encourage your children to pray even if they do not feel that they are good at it. Remind them that God is gentle and kind and always ready to hear their prayers and that God will never make fun of them for how they pray.*

Q: HOW CAN GOD HEAR OUR PRAYERS FROM HEAVEN?

JASON'S IMAGINATION

65

A: God can do anything. He is all-powerful and unlimited. He is everywhere all the time. He also knows everything. He knows what we think as well as what we say. So God can hear everyone's prayers from all over the world all the time.

Sometimes people think that God is "out there in heaven," far away. But God is not far away; he is always right here with us, living among his people.

KEY VERSE: *I am the Lord, the God of all the peoples of the world. Is anything too hard for me? (Jeremiah 32:27)*

RELATED VERSES: *Psalms 18:6; 116:1-2; 130:2; 139:2, 17-18*

RELATED QUESTIONS: *How does God listen? How does God hear prayers? Does God hear us when we pray? How can God hear what we say?*

Q: IF WE TALK TO GOD, DOES HE ALWAYS HEAR US?

66

A: Yes, God *always* hears us, no matter where we are or what we are doing. He is never asleep or far away. Nothing can stop him from hearing what we say.

God knows our thoughts, too. We do not have to talk loudly so that he can hear us. Even if we barely whisper or just think our prayer, God hears us.

But we also need to know that God hates sin. If we keep sin in our heart and try to hide it, God will want us to confess it first. He will hear our prayer, but he will be waiting to hear us confess our sin first. Then he will listen to our requests.

God loves us more than we could possibly imagine. He *wants* to hear from us. He is always available and always listening. We can talk to him anytime throughout the day.

KEY VERSES: *If I had not confessed the sin in my heart, my Lord would not have listened. But God did listen! He paid attention to my prayer. Praise God, who did not ignore my prayer and did not withdraw his unfailing love from me. (Psalm 66:18-20)*

RELATED VERSES: *Proverbs 15:29; Isaiah 55:6-7; 59:1-2; 1 Peter 3:12*

RELATED QUESTIONS: *Does God listen to you when you pray? Does God always hear you? Doesn't God always listen to our prayers? God is always listening, right?*

NOTE TO PARENTS: *Always present the positive side of what God knows, not just the negative. While it is true that the wicked cannot hide from God, it is just as true that God's people never have to fear his inattention. God is always ready and willing to hear our prayers. Comfort your children with this fact.*

HOW DOES GOD CONCENTRATE ON MILLIONS OF PEOPLE ALL PRAYING AT ONCE?

67

A: God is unlimited and all-powerful. He has no trouble hearing everyone's prayers all at once. Even human beings can do two things at once. People can ride a bike and notice things in the neighborhood at the same time. Yet God is far, far bigger and stronger than we are; he can easily do a million things at once. Also, he is everywhere at all times, and he knows everything. He knows what we think as well as what we say.

Always try to remember that we are different from God. He made us to be in one place at a time. He made us to think about one thing at a time. God is not limited in that way.

***

KEY VERSES: *What mighty praise, O God, belongs to you in Zion. We will fulfill our vows to you, for you answer our prayers, and to you all people will come. (Psalm 65:1-2)*

RELATED VERSES: *Psalm 139:4-6; Jeremiah 32:27; Romans 11:33-34*

RELATED QUESTIONS: *How can God hear so many people all at once? Doesn't it get a little noisy in his brain? Does God get headaches from everyone talking to him? Is he always listening? How can God give answers to everyone's prayers at once? How can God answer all the prayers if he's up in heaven?*

NOTE TO PARENTS: *It is important for our children to understand that the number of people who talk to God all at once does not diminish the amount of love and personal attention he gives each one. God is so awesome that when we pray we have his full love and attentiveness.*

Q: DOES GOD USUALLY GIVE US WHAT WE PRAY FOR?

68

A: Sometimes we pray for things that will hurt us or others, or we pray with a selfish attitude. It would not be good if God gave us what we asked for in those situations. At other times, what we want is good but not part of God's plan for us. Sometimes God wants us to wait—he may give us what we ask for, but not now. He knows that later is better.

But at other times, God does give us what we ask for because it is a good thing, and God loves to give us good things.

God has already told us how he will answer certain kinds of prayers. He promises to give us what we ask for whenever we ask for food, clothing, help living the Christian life, and wisdom. On the other hand, we know God will answer no whenever we ask for things that go against his will. We can be sure that God will always do what is best.

KEY VERSES: *He [Jesus] walked away, about a stone's throw, and knelt down and prayed, "Father, if you are willing, please take this cup of suffering away from me. Yet I want your will, not mine." (Luke 22:41-42)*

RELATED VERSES: *Psalm 17:6; Isaiah 55:8-9; Matthew 6:10; 7:11; Romans 11:36; James 1:5; 4:13-17*

RELATED QUESTIONS: *How many wishes do we get? Will God give you things from heaven that you wished for? Would God give somebody a home if they were poor? Would God supply me a home when I don't have one?*

NOTE TO PARENTS: *Encourage your children to ask God for specific things they are concerned about and to ask God for his will. Then encourage them to trust that God will take care of it. He is faithful and trustworthy.*

Q: DOES GOD ONLY GIVE US THINGS THAT WE NEED?

69

A: No, he gives us much more. The Bible says that every good thing we have comes from God (James 1:17). That includes all of the things that we need plus all of the extras that he so kindly gives to us. He is able to give us much more than we could possibly hope for or imagine (Ephesians 3:20).

God loves us and he delights in blessing us. Sometimes he lets us have more than what we need—good things that are just for us to enjoy.

Jesus put it this way: "You fathers—if your children ask for a fish, do you give them a snake instead? Or if they ask for an egg, do you give them a scorpion? Of course not! If you sinful people know how to give good gifts to your children, how much more will your heavenly Father give the Holy Spirit to those who ask him." (Luke 11:11-13)

KEY VERSES: *Praise the Lord, I tell myself, and never forget the good things he does for me. He fills my life with good things. My youth is renewed like the eagle's! (Psalm 103:2, 5)*

RELATED VERSES: *Exodus 23:25-26; Malachi 3:10; Ephesians 3:20; James 1:5, 17*

RELATED QUESTIONS: *If what the Bible says about "answering whatever we ask in Jesus' name" is true, why do my parents say he will only answer my need? How come I don't get candy when I pray for it?*

NOTE TO PARENTS: *Encourage your children to talk to God about fun stuff that is important to them, not merely "serious needs." God is interested in your children as they are. They will have plenty of serious topics to talk about soon enough.*

Q: WHY DOESN'T GOD GIVE US SOME THINGS WE PRAY FOR?

70

A: Because God is much wiser than we are. He knows what will happen if we get some of the things that we pray for. He can see all that is happening all over the world in every person's life all the time. He wants the very best for us. He has a plan for our lives and for the lives of every other person. So sometimes God does not give us what we pray for because it might hurt us or turn us the wrong way. At other times God doesn't give us something *right away*. He wants us to wait patiently for his timing. And sometimes God has plans that we cannot understand, so he waits or works something out that we cannot see.

Remember that God will never ignore our prayers. He loves us, hears our prayers, and works things out the best way possible. We can always trust in God's great care for us.

KEY VERSES: *Trust in the Lord with all your heart; do not depend on your own understanding. Seek his will in all you do, and he will direct your paths. (Proverbs 3:5-6)*

RELATED VERSES: *Genesis 21:1-2; Psalms 17:6; 40:1; James 1:6-7; 4:3; 1 Peter 5:7*

RELATED QUESTIONS: *Does God give us the things we want every time? Why doesn't God answer prayer when you ask for a puppy to be there when you wake up? Why doesn't God answer our questions sometimes?*

Q: HOW DO WE KNOW GOD IS ANSWERING OUR PRAYER?

IF THIS IS GOD ANSWERING MY PRAYER THIS MORNING, I AM SORRY I MISSED YOU. PLEASE LEAVE YOUR ANSWER AFTER THE BEEP AND I'LL CHAT WITH YOU AGAIN LATER ON THIS AFTERNOON.

71

A: We know that God is answering our prayers because God said in the Bible that he would. Of course, not all of his answers are yes. Sometimes God answers no. And sometimes he wants us to wait. The answer we receive is not always the one we had in mind, but it is always best.

God is most interested in changing us into his kind of people. That is his main goal for us. Prayer keeps us close to God and helps us understand what he wants us to become. We should pray knowing that God wants to hear from us and that his answer will be best.

KEY VERSE: *I took my troubles to the Lord; I cried out to him, and he answered my prayer. (Psalm 120:1)*

RELATED VERSES: *Psalms 17:6; 40:1; 119:26; 2 Corinthians 12:8-10; James 1:6-7*

RELATED QUESTIONS: *Why doesn't God answer every prayer? What does God say most—yes, no, or wait? When does God answer our prayers? How can we tell if God is telling us yes, no, or wait? Will God tell you yes or no?*

NOTE TO PARENTS: *Children tend to take life as it comes, without connecting events. They may not notice the many answers that God gives to their prayers. Watch for God's answers to your children's prayers. And when you see them, hold a little celebration and thank God together.*

Q: WHY DOESN'T GOD ANSWER PRAYERS RIGHT AWAY?

YES, OPERATOR – COULD YOU TELL ME THE TIME DIFFERENCE BETWEEN HERE AND HEAVEN? I AM EXPECTING AN IMPORTANT ANSWER TO PRAYER AND...

72

A: God knows more than we know. He has more wisdom than we have. So he gives the answer at the time that is best. Sometimes we do not have to wait at all—God answers our prayers even before we put them into words. At other times we must wait.

God has good reasons for his timing. Sometimes it takes awhile for the answer to come because God is using people and circumstances to answer, bringing them all together like a big team. Or God may know that we are not ready for the thing we want, so he spends a lot of time helping us grow and get ready.

And sometimes God waits to answer in order to test our faith and trust in him. He wants to see if we will keep trusting him even when it looks as if he is not answering. When we decide to keep trusting, our faith becomes stronger, and when the answer finally comes, that helps us trust God even more.

KEY VERSE: *There is a time for everything, a season for every activity under heaven. (Ecclesiastes 3:1)*

RELATED VERSES: *Genesis 21:1-2; 1 Kings 18:42-45; Psalms 40:1; 90:4; Isaiah 55:8-9; Luke 11:5-13; 2 Peter 3:9*

RELATED QUESTIONS: *Will the answer to my prayer be fast? What if we need what we're praying for right away? Do you sometimes get answers to prayer right away? Why does God wait to give you something? Would God answer your prayer quickly if you prayed for someone that was in the hospital?*

NOTE TO PARENTS: *Every child asks this question eventually. Encourage your children through this time to keep on trusting God. Together, ask God to help them keep trusting.*

Q: IF WE'RE DISCOURAGED AND IT SEEMS LIKE GOD DOESN'T ANSWER OUR PRAYERS, WHAT SHOULD WE DO?

PRAYER WAITING ROOM

73

A: We should keep on praying. If we are discouraged, we should tell him that we are discouraged. Then we should tell him that we know he is good and has not given up on us.

We should not blame God for our problems or for not answering our prayers. Sometimes bad things happen to test our faith or to make our faith stronger. We should remember that God is teaching us. God will give us strength to keep praying and to keep trusting that he is working things out for good.

Sometimes we are expecting things to work out a certain way. Often God answers in a way we are not expecting. We need to keep looking for his answers.

KEY VERSES: *One day Jesus told his disciples a story to illustrate their need for constant prayer and to show them that they must never give up. Then the Lord said, "Learn a lesson from this evil judge. Even he rendered a just decision in the end, so don't you think God will surely give justice to his chosen people who plead with him day and night? Will he keep putting them off?" (Luke 18:1, 6-7)*

RELATED VERSES: *Luke 11:5-13; Romans 8:28-29; Ephesians 6:18; James 1:2-7*

RELATED QUESTIONS: *Is God trying to teach us something when he doesn't answer right away? Why doesn't God give us what we need right away? How do you know God is talking to you when you pray? Once I prayed for a dog and never got one. Why?*

NOTE TO PARENTS: *When your children are waiting for God to answer their prayers, encourage them by reminding them of times when God has answered past prayers (both theirs and yours).*

Q: WHEN WE PRAY FOR SOMEONE NOT TO DIE AND THEN THEY DIE, DOES THAT MEAN THAT GOD DIDN'T LOVE THEM?

74

A: No, not at all. Every person has to die. That is part of life. When a person dies, it does not mean that God does not love the person or that God does not love the people who wanted that person to live. It also does not mean that someone lacked faith.

The Bible says that God loves *all* people. That is why he sent Jesus to die on the cross. He loved people so much that he sent Jesus to take away the sin of the world.

God hates death, but death is not the end. God's people can look forward to eternal life in heaven with God.

It is OK to cry when our loved ones die. We miss them very much. But if they are Christians, they are going to heaven, and that is much better for them.

KEY VERSE: *The Lord's loved ones are precious to him; it grieves him when they die. (Psalm 116:15)*

RELATED VERSES: *John 3:16; 1 Thessalonians 4:13-18*

RELATED QUESTIONS: *Does God's will always work out for good? Why won't God give you everything you want? How come, when we really pray hard for someone who is sick, they sometimes get worse? Why does God let people die? Does God answer all prayer?*

NOTE TO PARENTS: *Whenever your family prays for someone who is very ill and may die, commit that person to God's care. Ask together that God will do what is best for that person. Ask him also to help friends and family members help and comfort one another.*

Q: IF GOD HAS IT ALL PLANNED, CAN WE REALLY CHANGE IT BY PRAYING FOR THINGS?

75

A: The Bible says that God knows everything, even the future. Nothing takes him by surprise. And he is in control of the world. He rules it all.

Yet we also know that we work with God to accomplish his work. He could do it all without our prayers, but he has chosen not to. Our prayers are part of the way God's work will get done. Prayer is his idea. God wants his people to be coworkers with him in this world, and that means we must pray.

No one can see how their prayers affect God. It is better to pray in faith that God will do what is good than not to pray because we think that it might not make any difference. The main reason for praying is for us to get to know God better and to let him teach and care for us, not just to change things.

KEY VERSE: *The earnest prayer of a righteous person has great power and wonderful results. (James 5:16)*

RELATED VERSES: *Exodus 32:11, 14; Isaiah 55:8-9; Mark 14:36; Romans 8:28-29; James 4:13-17*

RELATED QUESTIONS: *If God knows and can give everything, why can't we have whatever we want? Is God's will different for everyone? What happens if you lose something and pray and it doesn't show up? Why don't I get it when I ask for money? How come God doesn't give you games? How come when we pray for something we want, we only get what we need?*

NOTE TO PARENTS: *Whenever a question like this comes up, remind your children why we pray. We pray to get to know God better and to invite God to change us. That is, we should conform more to God's will, not expect God to conform more to ours.*

Q: WHY DOES GOD NOT ANSWER OUR PRAYERS THE WAY WE WANT?

DAD, I GOT THE SNOW I PRAYED FOR, BUT IT'S NOT THE RIGHT KIND. IT DOESN'T MAKE SNOWBALLS.

76

A: God can see into the future, and knows the needs of every person everywhere at all times, so sometimes his answers seem strange to us. He sees what we cannot. Sometimes he answers our prayers exactly as we expect; sometimes the answer is so different that we hardly recognize it.

Sometimes God gives us what we were *really* asking for rather than the specific thing we thought we wanted. Maybe we asked for a toy but really we needed to be happy. God may make us happy *without* the toy, or he may send us a friend to play with instead.

If we trust in God's perfect love, we will always be content with his answers to our prayers.

KEY VERSES: *Dear friends, if our conscience is clear, we can come to God with bold confidence. And we will receive whatever we request because we obey him and do the things that please him. (1 John 3:21-22)*

RELATED VERSES: *Isaiah 55:8-9; Romans 8:28-29; Ephesians 3:20; 1 John 5:14-15*

RELATED QUESTIONS: *Why would God give us something we don't want? How come I always get sweaters and stuff for Christmas when I pray for toys? I have prayed for many things, but God hasn't given them to me. Why? Why doesn't God grant what we want? Because I thought he was supposed to make us happy.*

NOTE TO PARENTS: *Sometimes we are amazed at how God answers our prayers, but other times the answer comes so subtly that we wonder if God really did it or it just happened. Encourage your children with the fact that God is everywhere, knows everything, and is in control. If you prayed about it, God arranged it, subtly or miraculously.*

IF WE PRAY FOR SOMETHING ONE NIGHT, DO WE HAVE TO PRAY FOR IT THE NEXT NIGHT?

77

A: We do not have to keep praying the same prayers over and over, but it is good to pray every day for the things that really matter to us. It is all right to keep praying for the same thing when we don't see an answer and when it is important. Also, continuing to pray for the same thing has a way of changing us. While we are praying, God may show us a different direction to take or a new attitude to have. God uses prayer to change us. So it is good to keep praying for what matters to us.

KEY VERSE: *Be glad for all God is planning for you. Be patient in trouble, and always be prayerful. (Romans 12:12)*

RELATED VERSES: *Luke 18:1-8; Acts 1:14; Ephesians 6:18*

RELATED QUESTIONS: *Is it wrong to stop praying when you get tired of praying about the same thing every day? Should you pray for the same thing every time? Why does God not give us something until we've prayed enough? Why do people say prayers again and again? Why would God answer your prayer the fifth time you pray but not the first? If we keep on praying about something, will God answer our prayer? Does God answer prayers that have been said over and over again? Why should we not keep silent until God answers our prayer? Do people have to keep on praying and give God no rest?*

NOTE TO PARENTS: *The Bible tells us what we should pray for regularly (see questions 26–29 and the section "What to Pray For"). Help your children learn and add new kinds of prayers one at a time. Suggest topics (a little different each time) that will help them add to their prayer life slowly and progressively.*

Q: HOW COME GOD ANSWERS SOME PEOPLE'S PRAYERS AND NOT OTHERS?

78

A: God answers the prayers of the people who love him. The Bible says, "The earnest prayer of a righteous person has great power and wonderful results" (James 5:16). This verse teaches that a person who knows God and obeys him prays the kinds of prayers that God answers.

But not everyone in the world is part of God's family. Only people who have put their faith in Jesus are God's children. People who do not know God may pray, but they do not have the assurance that God will act on their request.

In the end, no one knows why God does what he does. God has plans for every person's life, and he works out those plans in his wisdom. We trust that his plans for us are good, and we trust that his plans for others are good too. We should not judge people or pretend to know why God does something for this person but not for that one.

KEY VERSE: *The Lord hates the sacrifice of the wicked, but he delights in the prayers of the upright. (Proverbs 15:8)*

RELATED VERSES: *Psalm 17:1; Luke 18:9-14; Hebrews 5:7; James 5:16*

RELATED QUESTIONS: *Does God answer everybody's prayers? Does God give us things if we're good or bad? Why do people think that God will listen to other people more than them?*

NOTE TO PARENTS: *Children tend to think that God rewards good people with answered prayer and punishes bad people with unanswered prayer. Remind your children that God answers prayers out of his love and grace. He does not use our works to determine who gets this or that blessing.*

WHY DO SOME PEOPLE WRITE DOWN WHEN GOD ANSWERS THEIR PRAYER?

79

A: Usually people write down God's answers to prayer because they want to remember how God has blessed them. Many passages in the Bible tell about people who did this. These people wrote down what God did for them in the past so that they would not forget and so their children would know about it too.

When we remember what God has done for us, we can thank and praise him. We can also be encouraged to keep praying and to live for him. It helps to go back and read about all the times just like this one when God answered prayers for which we patiently waited, especially if it looks as if God is not answering our prayers now.

KEY VERSE: *Think of the wonderful works he has done, the miracles and the judgments he handed down. (Psalm 105:5)*

RELATED VERSES: *Deuteronomy 6:12; Psalm 63:6*

RELATED QUESTIONS: *If we wrote it in a book every time God answered prayer, would we find that God always answers our prayers at some time or another? Is it wrong to not record it when God answers your prayer? Does God always answer prayer? Will God answer our prayers?*

NOTE TO PARENTS: *You can help your children make a "faith story" book for themselves and record in it the details of God's answering prayer. You might want to do one for the whole family.*

80

A: God answers our prayers in many ways. God is all-powerful, so he can use anything he wants to work out his plans. One of the ways he answers prayer is by using other people. For example, God often uses doctors and medicines to bring healing. He uses generous Christians to give money to people in need, in answer to their prayers.

God also uses other means. Sometimes he uses angels to do miracles or to intervene in some invisible way. He also uses events and the forces in nature.

Sometimes God simply changes *us*. For example, we may ask for more money, and God may answer by showing us how to use what we have more carefully. In other words, God gives us wisdom and teaches us; he works inside us to make us more like Christ in the way we think, talk, and act.

KEY VERSE: *You faithfully answer our prayers with awesome deeds, O God our savior. You are the hope of everyone on earth, even those who sail on distant seas. (Psalm 65:5)*

RELATED VERSES: *Psalms 81:7; 118:5-21; Daniel 10:12-14; 1 Corinthians 12:6-7; 2 Corinthians 1:11; Philemon 1:22*

RELATED QUESTIONS: *How does God make your prayer requests come true? Will candy fall out of the sky if you pray for it? How can God care for everyone in the world in one day? Why can't we hear God answer? Why doesn't God talk to you when you pray? Why does God answer our prayers?*

NOTE TO PARENTS: *Our children need to know that nothing can stop God from answering their prayers and nothing is too big or too small for him to do. He is always able, and he is always willing to work things out for our good.*

Q: WHEN GOD SAYS WE CAN PRAY ABOUT ANYTHING, DOES HE REALLY MEAN ANYTHING?

DEAR GOD, ABOUT THAT TRAINED CIRCUS ELEPHANT I WANT...

81

A: God always means what he says, so indeed we can talk with him about anything at all—feelings, requests, questions, anything we can think of. God invites us to come to him with whatever is on our mind. This does not mean that we will *get* everything we ask for, but we can pray about anything.

Prayer is not magic. It is a talk with God, who is a person. What matters most is that we trust in God and do what he says.

KEY VERSES: *[Jesus said,] "You can ask for anything in my name, and I will do it, because the work of the Son brings glory to the Father. Yes, ask anything in my name, and I will do it!" (John 14:13-14)*

RELATED VERSES: *Matthew 18:19-20; John 16:23-24; Philippians 4:6-7; 1 Peter 5:7*

RELATED QUESTION: *Does God give you anything if you have enough faith?*

Q: DOES IT MATTER HOW MUCH FAITH WE HAVE?

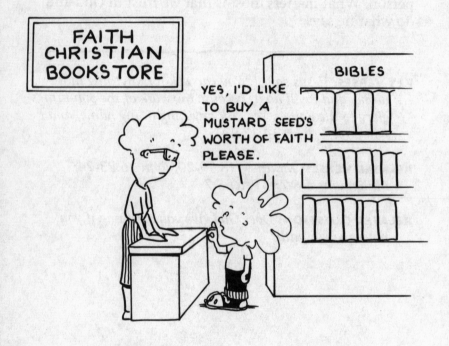

82

A: Jesus said that even if we have a very tiny amount of faith, we can accomplish great things in prayer. Having faith just means that we believe that God is faithful. In other words, we decide to trust that he loves us and will do what he said he would do. Great faith in God comes from having a little faith and deciding that God is faithful and that we are going to trust him no matter what.

We should put all our trust in God and depend on him, not on our own words, strength, or clever plans. If we trust even a little in our mighty God, it will make a huge difference.

KEY VERSE: *"You didn't have enough faith," Jesus told them. "I assure you, even if you had faith as small as a mustard seed you could say to this mountain, 'Move from here to there,' and it would move. Nothing would be impossible." (Matthew 17:20)*

RELATED VERSES: *Psalm 22:4-5; Mark 9:22-24; Luke 17:6; James 1:6-7*

RELATED QUESTIONS: *Is there ever enough faith? Why do people think if they have enough faith in God they will get anything? Why do people think that one way or another they can get whatever they want when it is not true?*

NOTE TO PARENTS: *A man wanted Jesus to heal his son. Jesus said, "Anything is possible if a person believes." The man replied, "I do believe, but help me not to doubt!" (Mark 9:23-24). Jesus healed his son. Sometimes we, like that man, doubt God. Whenever this happens with your children, let them know that God loves them and is willing to act on their behalf. Then lead them in asking God to overcome their doubt.*

Q: HOW DO WE KNOW WHO TO PRAY FOR?

YES, IS THIS THE UNITED NATIONS? I WAS WONDERING IF YOU HAD ANY PRAYER CONCERNS YOU'D LIKE TO SHARE?

83

A: We should pray for whomever we care about, and we should also pray for people in need, for pastors and missionaries, for government leaders, and for ourselves. For example, we can pray for family and friends. We can pray for people that we know are having trouble. We can pray for the pastor of our church, for the missionaries that our church supports, and for our Bible teachers. We can pray for our elected leaders, judges, lawmakers, school board superintendents, teachers, and other leaders. We can even make a list and pray for them regularly.

It is always good to pray for ourselves. We can ask God to teach us, to give us wisdom each day, and to make us grow in our faith.

KEY VERSES: *I urge you, first of all, to pray for all people. As you make your requests, plead for God's mercy upon them, and give thanks. Pray this way for kings and all others who are in authority, so that we can live in peace and quietness, in godliness and dignity. (1 Timothy 2:1-2)*

RELATED VERSES: *John 17:1-26; Romans 8:26; Colossians 1:3, 9-12; 1 Thessalonians 5:25; James 5:13-16*

RELATED QUESTIONS: *Can you pray for anyone, anywhere? Do a lot of people always have to pray for one person? Why doesn't God always make miracles?*

Q: HOW DOES PRAYING HELP SICK PEOPLE FEEL BETTER?

DRINK PLENTY OF FLUIDS,
GET LOTS OF REST, TAKE
TWO ASPIRIN AND PRAY
ONCE EVERY HOUR.

84

A: Sometimes God answers our prayers for a sick person by causing the person to get better. Perhaps we pray that the doctors will have wisdom, and God makes them think of a treatment that cures the disease.

Other times God helps the sick person learn to live with the illness. Perhaps the person cannot walk, but God teaches the person how to be joyful with God's love and care instead of walking again. Or the person becomes kind and caring toward others who are suffering because of what he or she has gone through.

One kind of healing makes the person's *body* better, and the other kind makes the *person* better. So praying for sick people is very important.

KEY VERSES: *Are any among you sick? They should call for the elders of the church and have them pray over them, anointing them with oil in the name of the Lord. And their prayer offered in faith will heal the sick, and the Lord will make them well. And anyone who has committed sins will be forgiven. (James 5:14-15)*

RELATED VERSES: *Psalms 103:1-5; 147:3; Isaiah 38:1-8; James 1:2-4*

RELATED QUESTIONS: *If you're sick, is it selfish to pray that you'll get better? Is it bad to not pray for someone who is sick? How can God touch someone? Why do people call the elders to pray for them?*

NOTE TO PARENTS: *Prayer is a natural response to sickness. Encourage your children to pray for people who are sick, but be sure to explain that the outcome is in God's hands.*

Q: HOW COME MISSIONARIES NEED SO MUCH PRAYER?

85

A: Because their work is very important, and they often run into problems that make their work difficult. They are telling people about Jesus. Only God can change people's minds and hearts. So we pray that God will open the hearts of people to the gospel message that the missionaries are telling. It is very important that people hear and understand the message of Jesus.

At the same time, missionary work is very difficult. Satan does not want missionaries to succeed in what they do. He will give the missionaries trouble and problems that make their work frustrating. For example, some people may speak against the missionaries. Or the missionaries may get sick. So we pray that God will keep Satan away from the missionaries and make them strong and able to do their work.

Missionaries depend on our prayers. If we do not pray, they will have a very hard time telling others about Christ.

KEY VERSES: *Don't forget to pray for us, too, that God will give us many opportunities to preach about his secret plan—that Christ is also for you Gentiles. That is why I am here in chains. Pray that I will proclaim this message as clearly as I should. (Colossians 4:3-4)*

RELATED VERSES: *Romans 15:31; Ephesians 6:19-20*

RELATED QUESTIONS: *Why do missionaries need people to pray for them? Why should you pray for missionaries?*

NOTE TO PARENTS: *Try to introduce your children to at least one missionary. The best candidates are missionaries who are relationally close to you or are from your church. Go hear them speak at your church the next time you have opportunity to do so. You can also open your home to missionaries who are on furlough. Kids find it easier to pray for people they know than for strangers.*

Q: WHAT DO PRAYER WARRIORS DO?

86

A: Some people use the term "prayer warriors" to describe people who seem to pray all the time. They pray for others and for God's work on a regular basis. They know that prayer is important. Because they care about God's work in the world, they make sure that they pray about it often.

God wants all of us to pray for others, for Christian leaders, and for the growth of his kingdom. But some people feel that God has given them an extra special task of spending a lot of time doing this.

KEY VERSE: *Timothy, I thank God for you. He is the God I serve with a clear conscience, just as my ancestors did. Night and day I constantly remember you in my prayers. (2 Timothy 1:3)*

RELATED VERSES: *Daniel 6:10; Luke 2:36-37; Acts 6:3-4; 1 Thessalonians 3:10; 5:17*

RELATED QUESTIONS: *What are intercessory prayers? What makes someone a better pray-er? Are prayer warriors and intercessors the same thing? What does "intercessory prayer" mean? What are intercessors, and why do we need them? Who are prayer warriors? Why do some people call themselves prayer warriors?*

Q: WHAT SHOULD A PERSON DO WHO FEELS EMBARRASSED TO PRAY IN PUBLIC?

PUBLIC PRAYER PRACTISE

87

A: It is OK to pray in public as long as we are not showing off. We should not feel ashamed of it or embarrassed. But some people are shy. When they are asked to pray aloud, they feel very awkward. They are afraid that they will say something wrong and that people will laugh at them.

We must remember that we do not pray to impress others. Whatever we pray is all right if it comes from the heart. So when we are asked to pray in public, we can just talk to God in our own words and in our own way.

KEY VERSE: *Then I will declare the wonder of your name to my brothers and sisters. I will praise you among all your people. (Psalm 22:22)*

RELATED VERSES: *Psalm 96:3; Matthew 6:5-6; Luke 9:26; Romans 1:16*

RELATED QUESTIONS: *What if your friends make fun of you if you pray in church? Do you have to pray if you are asked to pray? Are some people given the gift of being able to speak to God freely in front of others, while others stumble on words?*

NOTE TO PARENTS: *At a certain age, some children will become self-conscious about praying in public. You can teach them to pray in front of others (and help them get used to it) by having them take turns saying the mealtime prayer. Start simple, and expand it to include a current family issue or two.*

Q: IF WE DON'T LIKE WHAT SOMEONE PRAYED FOR, WHAT SHOULD WE DO?

88

A: Nothing. We should let people lead us in prayer and not judge them or what they say. Some people become used to certain patterns of praying that may seem strange to us. We should be careful not to scorn them just because we do not like their choice of words or style of praying. They may just have a different way of asking God for something. But remember that God cares most about the heart of the people praying, not the specific words they use.

Sometimes we can learn from others' prayers. If we do not like what someone prayed for, we should thank God that the person prayed and then think about what we can learn from the person's prayer. We should always be open to learning new things from others. We should especially be glad that they are praying.

KEY VERSE: *Stop judging others, and you will not be judged. Stop criticizing others, or it will all come back on you. If you forgive others, you will be forgiven. (Luke 6:37)*

RELATED VERSES: *Matthew 7:1-5; Romans 14:10-13*

RELATED QUESTIONS: *Why do you have to pray together in a church? I thought the people made up the church, not the building. Do you have to pray in church? Why do people pray in church?*

Q: WHY DOES GOD WANT US TO PRAY TOGETHER?

89

A: God enjoys it when his people pray together because it is one of the ways we can help and support one another. The Bible calls Christians a "body." This means that they work best when they work together, like the different parts of a body. When believers pray together, they strengthen and encourage each other. They complement each other. And they can share prayer requests and pray for each other. It is powerful.

KEY VERSES: *[Jesus said,] "I also tell you this: If two of you agree down here on earth concerning anything you ask, my Father in heaven will do it for you. For where two or three gather together because they are mine, I am there among them." (Matthew 18:19-20)*

RELATED VERSES: *2 Chronicles 7:14; Psalm 34:3*

RELATED QUESTIONS: *Why does God like us to pray with other people? Why do people pray together at church but sometimes not at home? Why do a lot of people pray when there's a real need or someone is sick?*

NOTE TO PARENTS: *Always be ready to pray with your children. When they have a need or you both see a need, pray about it together. Ask your children to pray for you, too, and give them specifics. Also let your children know that you are praying for them.*

Q: DO CHILDREN HAVE TO PRAY WITH AN ADULT?

I'M GOING TO PRAY FOR SOME REALLY BIG THINGS! I THINK IT WOULD HELP IF YOU FILLED OUT THIS CONSENT FORM.

90

A: Not at all. Jesus said, "Let the children come to me. Don't stop them!" (Luke 18:16). Any believer, no matter how old or young, can talk with God alone. God loves to hear from his children. He welcomes all sincere prayers.

Go ahead and practice praying to God all by yourself. You can start by telling him what is on your mind and asking him to help you solve your problems. You can also ask him to teach you to pray better. You do not have to do it a certain way; it is like talking to your friends— you just tell them what you want to say in your own words. Then thank God for understanding what you want to say, even if you don't know how to say it.

KEY VERSE: *You have taught children and nursing infants to give you praise. (Psalm 8:2)*

RELATED VERSES: *Matthew 6:6; 19:13-15; Luke 18:16; Romans 8:26-27*

RELATED QUESTIONS: *Should you pray alone? Is it OK to pray alone? Is it bad to pray alone all the time? Do you have to pray with anybody? Do you have to pray by yourself? Why do some kids think they have to pray with an adult?*

NOTE TO PARENTS: *When your children start praying on their own, you have successfully primed the pump. But do not leave them there. Continue getting together with them for prayer so that you can continue to help them while also encouraging them to pray on their own. If there is something they want to pray about privately, without your hearing it, don't pry it out of them; encourage it. It shows that they are starting to trust God with private and important concerns. That is very good.*

Q: IS GROUP PRAYER MORE POWERFUL?

EMERGENCY
PRAYER MEETING
PLACE: Here
TIME: NOW!

91

A: It can be. Group prayer can be more powerful than individual prayer because it helps believers grow closer to each other as well as closer to God. It gets a lot of people praying for the same thing. It is also a great way of showing God that we agree about what is important.

Group prayer is one way God helps us. We may not feel like praying, or we may not feel very confident in our prayers. So others pray with us to help us receive God's strength and help. In that way it is more powerful because we can get our prayers answered even when we are feeling weak.

KEY VERSE: *And let us not neglect our meeting together, as some people do, but encourage and warn each other, especially now that the day of his coming back again is drawing near. (Hebrews 10:25)*

RELATED VERSES: *Matthew 18:19-20; Acts 1:14*

RELATED QUESTIONS: *Can we pray by ourselves? What about the people who pray alone? I think it's OK to pray for yourself, and God will listen, but is it better to get more people involved? It's good to have a lot of people, but why do you have to have so-o-o many people to make the prayer more powerful? Is it bad to pray by yourself?*

NOTE TO PARENTS: *A good time to teach your children the importance of group prayer is when your family is going through a tough time. You can call the family together, explain the situation and what you want to tell God, and then pray together.*

Q: WHY DO SOME PEOPLE HOLD HANDS WHILE THEY'RE PRAYING?

92

A: Holding hands with others when we pray can help us feel together and more like we care for each other. Also, holding hands can be a sign that we all agree in what we are talking to God about. People in a family or small group do not have to hold hands when they pray together, but sometimes they like to.

KEY VERSES: *May God, who gives this patience and encouragement, help you live in complete harmony with each other—each with the attitude of Christ Jesus toward the other. Then all of you can join together with one voice, giving praise and glory to God, the Father of our Lord Jesus Christ. (Romans 15:5-6)*

RELATED VERSE: *1 Corinthians 1:10*

RELATED QUESTIONS: *Does holding hands increase the power of prayer? When people pray together and hold hands, isn't that because they are really agreeing? Why do we hold hands and close our eyes when we pray? Does it mean anything to hold hands while we pray?*

NOTE TO PARENTS: *Holding hands when you are praying with your children can help them concentrate and not fidget so much. But also let your children know that holding hands is not essential.*

Q: DO WE HAVE TO PRAY EVERY NIGHT?

93

A: No. God has not set exact times when we *must* pray. Prayer is simply something that we should do every day. A lot of people like to pray every night and try to keep that habit because they know that prayer is important, and the end of the day seems to be a good time for them. Others prefer to pray in the morning before they start the day. Some people set aside special time to pray in the middle of the day. Praying at night is a good habit, but it is not a rule that we have to follow. Each of us should pick the time of day that works best for us.

KEY VERSE: *Timothy, I thank God for you. He is the God I serve with a clear conscience, just as my ancestors did. Night and day I constantly remember you in my prayers. (2 Timothy 1:3)*

RELATED VERSES: *Psalms 42:8; 55:17; 119:147-148*

RELATED QUESTIONS: *Why do we pray every night? Do you have to pray at night?*

NOTE TO PARENTS: *As your children get older, they may want to change the time of their devotional prayer. Encourage them to pray during a part of the day when they can concentrate and be consistent.*

Q: WHAT IF GOD HAS ALREADY ANSWERED ALL OF OUR PRAYERS?

94

A: First of all, we can thank him for answering them! We can be glad, tell God thank you, and praise him for being so good to us. Then we can tell someone else about it so they know about the great things God has done for us. And then we should think about new requests we can bring to him. If we cannot think of anything *we* need, we can think of other people who need prayer. We can pray for the people in our family, for our friends, for our leaders, and even for our enemies. Then we can pray for wisdom and that God will teach us new things. There's always something to talk to God about.

KEY VERSES: *Give thanks to the Lord, for he is good! His faithful love endures forever. Has the Lord redeemed you? Then speak out! Tell others he has saved you from your enemies. (Psalm 107:1-2)*

RELATED VERSES: *Psalm 118:21; Philippians 4:4; James 5:13-18*

RELATED QUESTION: *What if we have absolutely no prayer requests or praise reports?*

NOTE TO PARENTS: *Encourage your children to tell God what is on their mind even if they don't have a request to make. As they get older and develop their relationship with God, they will get more comfortable with different kinds of prayer. And when you pray with them, let them hear you talk to God about what is on your mind so that they can see that not all prayer has to involve a list of needs.*

Q: IF WE'VE PRAYED ALL THROUGH THE DAY, DO WE STILL NEED TO PRAY AT NIGHT?

OPEN 9:30 – ~~5:00~~
~~6:00~~
~~7:30~~
~~9:00~~

OR CALL DIRECT

JASON'S
PRAYER
BOOTH

95

A: We should try not to think of prayer as a requirement that we have to meet. Instead, we should make a habit of praying. We should pray about things that matter to us. And we should pray honestly and privately.

Remember that prayer is an opportunity to talk to God, who knows us and loves us. If we know him and love him, we will pray often because we know he is on our side. We will pray simply because we love God. But we will not worry whether we have prayed enough.

Bedtime is a good time to pray because we can think through the day and pray about the next day. But we do not need to think of bedtime prayer as a chore to do. If we have already spoken with God about our concerns, we can just thank him for taking care of us as we drift off to sleep.

KEY VERSE: *Keep on praying. (1 Thessalonians 5:17)*

RELATED VERSES: *Psalm 55:17; Luke 2:37; Ephesians 6:18*

RELATED QUESTIONS: *What would happen if you didn't pray at night? Why do we have to say a prayer before we go to bed? Why do you have to pray at night?*

NOTE TO PARENTS: *Do not force children to pray. Always present prayer as an opportunity to do something good and pleasing to you and to God. This will help your children see prayer as a positive activity that they can do.*

Q: ARE YOUR DAYTIME PRAYERS AS EFFECTIVE AS YOUR NIGHT ONES?

96

A: God does not hear prayers better during the day than during the night. And God does not care what time of day we choose to pray. What God cares about is our attitude. He wants our prayers to be honest and heartfelt—he wants us to say what is on our mind.

Some people find it easier to pray at night than during the day. Perhaps they become more easily distracted during the day, thinking about all the things they have to do and the places they have to go. They may have trouble concentrating on their prayer during the day. For them, praying at night may be better.

Others find it easier to pray during the day because they become drowsy at night. They cannot concentrate on praying at night because they too quickly fall asleep.

It is always good to pray, whether it is nighttime or daytime. God always loves to hear from us.

KEY VERSE: *Night and day we pray earnestly for you, asking God to let us see you again to fill up anything that may still be missing in your faith. (1 Thessalonians 3:10)*

RELATED VERSES: *Mark 1:35; Luke 6:12; 2 Timothy 1:3*

RELATED QUESTION: *Why is there a set time to pray?*

Q:
AFTER OUR PARENTS PRAY WITH US, DO WE STILL NEED TO PRAY ON OUR OWN LATER?

97

A: We certainly can. We do not have to pray only with our parents. If we have our own private requests that we want to bring to God, we should go ahead and do so. It is OK to tell God whatever we like. He loves us and cares for us and loves to hear anything and everything we want to say to him, as long as it is respectful.

But we do not have to pray on our own in order for God to love us or to answer our requests. If we happen to pray mostly with our parents, God does not mind. The important thing is that we pray.

KEY VERSES: *Jesus said, "Let the children come to me. Don't stop them! For the Kingdom of Heaven belongs to such as these." And he put his hands on their heads and blessed them before he left. (Matthew 19:14-15)*

RELATED VERSES: *Luke 18:15-17*

RELATED QUESTIONS: *I think praying with parents is good, but what if you have a personal prayer and want to be alone? Why do we have to pray with our parents? Why do parents pray with us on a regular basis instead of just once in a while? Do you have to pray with your mom and dad? Why do parents pray with children?*

NOTE TO PARENTS: *It is great for you to pray with your children; it lets you lead them to God and teach them how to pray. But be sure your children also know that God welcomes their private prayers. If they are afraid of "not saying it right," tell them that God is very happy with the way they pray all by themselves and that he will help them grow. Remind them that Jesus welcomes children.*

Q: WHY ARE WE SOMETIMES FORCED TO PRAY? SHOULDN'T WE PRAY WHEN WE WANT TO?

98

A: Prayer is a good thing to do, just like brushing our teeth, taking a bath, and eating good food. We may not always enjoy praying, but we should do it whether we feel like it or not.

Sometimes parents make children pray even if they don't feel like it or want to. There is nothing wrong with that. If we always waited till we *felt* like eating good food, we would probably eat nothing but cookies and ice cream. Then we would get sick, fat, and weak. We simply need to do what we ought to do. This is true of prayer, too. And prayer is much more important than eating good food, taking a bath, or anything else.

The good news is that God rewards those who discipline themselves to pray. They soon find that they miss it when they cannot do it. God changes us as we pray, and that is just one more reason we should work at it.

KEY VERSE: *Devote yourselves to prayer with an alert mind and a thankful heart. (Colossians 4:2)*

RELATED VERSES: *Colossians 3:17; 1 Thessalonians 5:17-18*

RELATED QUESTIONS: *Why do our parents remind us to pray? Why do parents tell us to pray when we are bad? Why do parents make us pray when we already have? It drives me crazy!*

NOTE TO PARENTS: *Be careful never to use prayer as a punishment. Do not make children pray as penance or as a way of making them think about God. Make prayer something to look forward to. And if they do not want to pray, tell them that's OK, and pray for them aloud as they listen. Lead them; do not push them.*

Q: HOW CAN WE THINK OF SOMETHING GOOD TO PRAY ABOUT IF WE'VE HAD A BAD DAY?

99

A: Even when we have had a terrible day, we have good things to pray about. For example, God is good—we can thank him for being good, for being in control, and for caring about us. We can tell God about our bad day and what makes us upset about it. Then we can ask him to help us with our bad situation. Also, we can express confidence in God's goodness and in his willingness to help us. We can say that we are glad he is with us.

Praying and praising God is a good way to take our mind off our troubles.

KEY VERSE: *No matter what happens, always be thankful, for this is God's will for you who belong to Christ Jesus. (1 Thessalonians 5:18)*

RELATED VERSES: *Psalms 43:1-5; 69:16-18; James 1:2-4*

RELATED QUESTIONS: *Why should you thank God for a good day if you had a bad day? Why do we have to pray even if we are in a bad mood? Is it bad not to pray even if you are in a bad mood? If we have a bad day, will God still forgive us if we don't pray? Why do we thank God when we've had a bad day? Do we have to thank God for the day, or could we ask him for other things instead?*

NOTE TO PARENTS: *It is very reassuring to a child for Mom or Dad to pray for him or her. Whenever your children have a bad day, pray for them. Express sadness at the things that have made your children sad, ask God to help, and express confidence that he will help. This will do more to calm and comfort them than making them pray.*

Q: DO WE HAVE TO PRAY EVEN IF WE'RE TIRED?

100

A: Just before Jesus was arrested, he asked his disciples to stay awake and pray, but they fell asleep. It is difficult to pray when we are tired, but we should not let tiredness keep us from talking with God. We should try hard to make a habit of praying, even if it is sometimes inconvenient.

KEY VERSE: *"Why are you sleeping?" he asked. "Get up and pray. Otherwise temptation will overpower you." (Luke 22:46)*

RELATED VERSES: *Proverbs 6:6-11; Mark 14:37-38; Luke 6:12*

RELATED QUESTIONS: *Will God punish us if we're too tired to pray at night and our parents told us to? Does it matter if you're too tired to pray at night? God already knows everything.*

NOTE TO PARENTS: *If your children are too tired to pray, pray for them and let them go to sleep. Tired children do not learn well. And if your children are often too tired to pray, consider changing your family's bedtime routine so they are more awake at prayer time.*

Q: IS IT BAD TO FALL ASLEEP WHEN WE ARE PRAYING TO GOD?

101

A: No, it is not bad to fall asleep while praying. In fact, there is no better way to fall asleep. If we are in bed and want to talk to God until we fall asleep, that is a wonderful thing to do. It is always good to pray.

But if we are falling asleep because we pray *only* when we are tired, then we need to find another time to pray so we can also pray when we are awake. It is always good to set aside times for prayer when we can think clearly and not get distracted.

KEY VERSE: *Through each day the Lord pours his unfailing love upon me, and through each night I sing his songs, praying to God who gives me life. (Psalm 42:8)*

RELATED VERSES: *Psalms 3:5; 4:8; 63:6; Matthew 26:39-45*

RELATED QUESTIONS: *When people fall asleep when they're praying, does God know what they would have prayed if they had stayed awake? Some people pray, and in the middle of praying they fall asleep. Why? Why do people fall asleep right in the middle of a prayer? Does it really matter if people fall asleep in the middle of their prayers? Because God knows everything! Is God mad when people fall asleep during prayer?*

Q: HOW COME SOME PEOPLE ARE ASKING FOR SUNSHINE WHILE OTHER PEOPLE ARE ASKING FOR RAIN?

102

A: People ask God for different things because they have different needs and different concerns. A baseball player might ask God for sunshine so she can play her game. At the same time, a farmer nearby might ask God for rain to help his crops to grow. Fortunately, God sees everything and knows what is best. He can work out all things everywhere for everyone's best because he is infinite and all-powerful. We can be thankful that God is wiser than we are and that he sees the whole picture, not just one part of it!

KEY VERSE: *For our God is in the heavens, and he does as he wishes. (Psalm 115:3)*

RELATED VERSES: *2 Samuel 15:25-26; Matthew 5:45; Romans 8:28-29; James 5:17-18*

RELATED QUESTIONS: *Does God just answer the prayer for the weather he wants? Who cares if it rains or shines? I don't; I'm thankful for every day. Shouldn't we just pray for God to give us the weather the land needs? Why do people ask for rain or sunshine? Why do people pray for rain?*

NOTE TO PARENTS: *Do not discourage your children from praying for things like weather just because the answers may not come as asked. Explain that God hears and cares but must consider what is best. Have them pray something like "God, if it is possible, I'd really like sunshine for our camping trip. But I trust you can work things out in another way too. Please work it out in the way that is best."*

Q: CAN WE PRAY FOR SNOW SO WE CAN'T GO TO SCHOOL?

103

A: We can talk with God about anything that is on our mind. But we should not make silly, selfish, or foolish requests. For example, we *could* pray that money would fall from the sky, but that would be both silly and selfish. Praying for school to be called off would be foolish. We should do what is good and wise, and that includes going to school. We should try to match our desires with God's. Instead of treating him like a genie, we should treat him like our loving Father and wise, almighty God.

KEY VERSE: *Take delight in the Lord, and he will give you your heart's desires. (Psalm 37:4)*

RELATED VERSES: *Matthew 6:9-10; Luke 22:41-42*

RELATED QUESTIONS: *Is it wrong to ask God to make it snow? Does it bug God if people always pray about snow or rain? Would God make snow in the summer?*

Q: DOES GOD ONLY ANSWER SERIOUS QUESTIONS?

104

A: God cares about us. He does not limit himself only to "major" problems, such as life-threatening illnesses, wars, and natural disasters. God tells us to bring *all* of our concerns to him. If something is important to us, we should talk to him about it. We should not try to guess what God is thinking or what he might approve of.

It is true that God does not want us to pray silly prayers. Prayer is not a joke. But God is always ready and willing to hear our honest concerns, no matter how "small" they may seem to us.

KEY VERSE: *Give all your worries and cares to God, for he cares about what happens to you. (1 Peter 5:7)*

RELATED VERSES: *Psalm 139:1-18; Philippians 4:4-10*

RELATED QUESTIONS: *Why is God so wonderful? Does God just answer the person that he feels like answering?*

NOTE TO PARENTS: *Encourage your children to pray about all of their concerns, no matter how small those concerns may be. If we reserve prayer for "serious" issues, we give the impression that we should pray only to get out of jams. We also make the mistake of assuming we know what is truly serious and what is not. All of our concerns are serious to God.*

Q: IS IT OK TO COMPLAIN TO GOD?

DEAR GOD, PLEASE HELP MY MOM, SHE'S GOING CLEAN CRAZY. IT'S "CLEAN YOUR ROOM, CLEAN YOUR HANDS"... I CAN UNDERSTAND THAT, BUT "CLEAN OUT YOUR GARBAGE CAN"? THAT'S WHAT A GARBAGE CAN IS FOR!

105

A: Yes, it is all right to complain to God. We should be honest about our feelings, and we certainly cannot hide them from God. Anyone who reads the Psalms and the book of Job can see that the people who prayed told God how they really felt. But they also did not accuse God of doing something wrong. They did not accuse him of losing control or of doing something bad. They told God that they believed in his goodness. That is how we should pray too.

We can and should tell God how we feel. Also, we should tell him that we know he is God and has our best interests in mind. We should thank him for loving us.

God is on our side. He will come alongside and help us if we trust him.

KEY VERSES: *How long, O Lord, must I call for help? But you do not listen! "Violence!" I cry, but you do not come to save. Must I forever see this sin and misery all around me? Wherever I look, I see destruction and violence. I am surrounded by people who love to argue and fight. (Habakkuk 1:2-3)*

RELATED VERSES: *Job 3:1-10; Psalms 77:1-20; 102:1-28; Ecclesiastes 7:13-14; Habakkuk 1:1–2:1; 1 Peter 5:7*

RELATED QUESTION: *Why can't we know everything when we're born?*

NOTE TO PARENTS: *There is a difference between complaining to God and lashing out at him in anger. Lead your children to see God as their ally, loving Father, and best friend. Lead them from their complaint to an expression of faith in God and trust in his goodness.*

Q: DOESN'T GOD EVER GET TIRED OF ANSWERING PRAYERS?

106

A: Nope. God never gets even a little bit tired of answering prayers. He loves to hear from us because he loves us. Jesus died for our sins so that we could have friendship with him. That does not change no matter how often we ask things of him.

God wants to work in our lives to change our behavior, thoughts, and habits. We should never fear that we are wearing him out with our prayers, even when we pray the same thing over and over. That is because he wants to keep being a part of our lives.

KEY VERSES: *O Israel, how can you say the Lord does not see your troubles? How can you say God refuses to hear your case? Have you never heard or understood? Don't you know that the Lord is the everlasting God, the Creator of all the earth? He never grows faint or weary. No one can measure the depths of his understanding. (Isaiah 40:27-28)*

RELATED VERSES: *Proverbs 15:8; Hebrews 4:14-16; 10:19-22; 1 Peter 5:7*

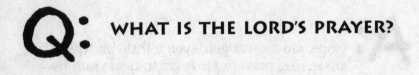

Q: WHAT IS THE LORD'S PRAYER?

107

A: It is a prayer that Jesus gave to his disciples when they asked him to teach them how to pray. Jesus did not call it the Lord's Prayer, but people since then have called it that. It gives a good model for all Christians to follow in their prayers. It tells us what kinds of things God wants us to focus our prayers on.

Take a look at the Lord's Prayer from time to time. It can give you ideas of what to pray for.

KEY VERSES: *Pray like this: Our Father in heaven, may your name be honored. May your Kingdom come soon. May your will be done here on earth, just as it is in heaven. Give us our food for today, and forgive us our sins, just as we have forgiven those who have sinned against us. And don't let us yield to temptation, but deliver us from the evil one. (Matthew 6:9-13)*

RELATED VERSES: *Luke 11:2-4*

RELATED QUESTIONS: *Why aren't there names for all prayers? What does* hallowed *mean? How can a kingdom come?*

Q: WHERE DID ANGELS COME FROM?

JASON'S IMAGINATION

108

A: God created everything, and that includes angels. The Bible doesn't say, "God created angels," nor does it mention when God created angels. But we know he did because the Bible explains that God created everything that exists. The Bible never says that God created dogs, for example, but we know that he did because he created all things. We also don't know if God created all the angels at once or if he creates them as he needs them. Angels take orders from God and serve him. They aren't equal with God and don't have the same powers as God. Remember, God didn't discover angels— he created them.

KEY VERSES: *Praise [God], all his angels, all the armies of heaven. . . . Let everything he has made give praise to him. For he gave the command, and they came into being. (Psalm 148:2, 5)*

RELATED VERSES: *Nehemiah 9:6; Colossians 1:15-16*

RELATED QUESTIONS: *On which of the seven days did God create the angels? How did God discover angels? Are angels like people except that they live in heaven? Do angels have mothers? How did God get the idea to make angels? How were angels made? Did God make angels?*

NOTE TO PARENTS: *Try to avoid using the word* angel *when it is inaccurate, such as calling your child a "little angel" or saying that a person who died has become an angel. These innocent explanations can easily confuse children.*

Q: DO ANGELS HAVE NAMES?

109

A: The Bible mentions two angels by name—Gabriel and Michael. We don't know if all angels have names, but they probably do since angels are personal beings, like people. Even though they don't have bodies, they have identities, just like people. But they're not human beings. They are God's servants. He created them to do his work. Remember, the only place that we can learn for sure about angels is in the Bible, God's Word.

KEY VERSE: *"Don't even ask my name," the Angel replied. "For it is a secret." (Judges 13:18)*

RELATED VERSES: *Daniel 8:16; 10:13; Luke 1:19, 26; Jude 1:9; Revelation 12:7*

RELATED QUESTIONS: *How does God remember all the angels? How come God only named two angels in the whole Bible? Was the angel's name beyond understanding because it was too hard to say (Judges 13:18)?*

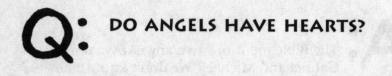

Q: DO ANGELS HAVE HEARTS?

To my
Guardian angel
my very special
valentine!
xoxoxo
from Jason
+ Max

110

A: If you're asking whether angels have feelings, the answer is yes. Angels have feelings just as people do and just as God does. Many Bible passages tell of angels *rejoicing* whenever someone first believes in Jesus. Others tell of angels singing songs of gladness and praise to God.

Angels can also think. The Bible says they can tell the difference between good and evil. Satan and his demons used to be good angels, but they chose to do evil. (More on that in question 24.) The Bible also says that angels care about us and that they helped Jesus.

But angels don't have real hearts because they don't have physical bodies.

KEY VERSE: *There is joy among the angels of God when one sinner repents. (Luke 15:10)*

RELATED VERSES: *2 Samuel 14:17, 20; Psalm 34:7; 91:11; Luke 2:13-14; Hebrews 12:22-23; Revelation 5:11-12*

RELATED QUESTION: *Do angels get angry?*

Q: DO ANGELS GROW UP?

111

A: You may have seen paintings or cartoons of "baby angels," but those are not true pictures of angels. Angels don't have physical bodies, so they are never born, they never grow up, and they never die. They don't need to eat or drink, and they don't outgrow their clothes. But they can learn—they can get more knowledge than they started with. The Bible says that angels learn from watching people (they "grow in knowledge"). Angels are learning more and more of God's wisdom all the time.

KEY VERSE: *[God] wanted to show all the rulers in Heaven how perfectly wise he is. They will see the Jews and Gentiles joined together in his Church. (Ephesians 3:10)*

RELATED VERSES: *Matthew 22:30; 1 Peter 1:12*

RELATED QUESTIONS: *Do angels live like we do today? Does God have to teach his angels to do things? Do angels have ages? Can angels have children? Do angels take care of themselves? Does God tell them stories?*

NOTE TO PARENTS: *We associate growth with change. That is, we talk about people "growing" spiritually, mentally, and in other areas to describe the changes we see happening in them. When children ask, "Do angels grow up?" however, they are usually referring to physical growth—aging and getting bigger, stronger, faster, etc.*

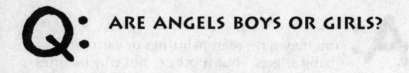

Q: ARE ANGELS BOYS OR GIRLS?

ANGEL
IN
DISGUISE

112

A: *People* are either male or female (boys or girls) because of their bodies—the way they are physically. But angels don't have physical bodies, so they are neither boys nor girls. (Jesus explained that angels don't get married.) The angels Michael and Gabriel have male names, but that doesn't mean that they are men. When angels visited people in human form (when Gabriel visited Mary, for example), usually it was as a man.

KEY VERSE: *For in the resurrection there is no marriage. Everyone is like the angels in Heaven. (Matthew 22:30)*

RELATED VERSES: *Mark 12:25; 16:5; Hebrews 1:14; 13:2*

RELATED QUESTIONS: *Are there girl angels, or are they all boys? When I die, will I become an angel?*

Q: DO ANGELS GET TIRED?

113

A: Angels never get tired, not even a little bit, and they never sleep. They don't need sleep like you do. Good angels are incredibly powerful and always ready to do what God tells them to do. Angels can open locked doors, roll away huge stones, and even wipe out whole armies. That's because they are God's servants, and God gives them the power they need to carry out his work. Angels are not all-powerful, though. The book of Daniel tells of a time when Satan stopped an angel for a little while, until the archangel Michael came to help him. But angels never get tired, weak, or sick. And someday they will fight in the final battle against Satan and his demons—and *win*.

KEY VERSE: *Suddenly there was a great earthquake. For an Angel of the Lord came down from Heaven. He rolled aside the stone and sat on it. (Matthew 28:2)*

RELATED VERSES: *Psalm 103:20; Daniel 9:21-23; 10:13; Acts 5:19; 2 Peter 2:11; Revelation 12:7-8*

RELATED QUESTIONS: *How can angels be so strong that they were able to keep the lions' mouths from closing? Do angels help out other angels? Just how strong are angels? Do angels sleep?*

Q: DO ALL ANGELS HAVE BLONDE HAIR?

114

A:

Actually, the Bible never says that angels have hair. Whenever the Bible describes them as appearing as people, it doesn't mention what color their hair is. Remember, angels don't have bodies like humans do. You may have seen paintings of angels with blonde hair, or you may have seen cartoons that show them that way, but we don't know exactly what angels looked like when they appeared to people. They *can* appear with blonde hair, but they don't have to. The Bible does say, however, that they often appeared as shining, radiant, or glorious beings. Maybe that's where people got the idea that they must have blonde hair. But then it would be just as likely that they had *red* hair. Right?

KEY VERSE: *The angels are your messengers. They are your servants of fire! (Psalm 104:4)*

RELATED VERSES: *Luke 2:9-10; John 20:12; Acts 12:7; 2 Thessalonians 1:7; Hebrews 1:7*

RELATED QUESTIONS: *What do angels look like? Are angels as bright as the sun? Are some angels black?*

Q: DO ANGELS HAVE HALOS?

115

A: Many drawings of angels or of people in the Bible show them with little rings of light over their heads that look a lot like round fluorescent light-bulbs. Those are called halos. But there is no evidence in the Bible that anyone, human or angel, ever had a halo. Real angels don't look anything like those pictures. Some passages in the Bible describe angels as very bright beings. Their clothes or their faces shine with bright light, glow like hot metal, or gleam like the sun. This is because angels reflect the glory of God. (When Moses met with God on Mount Sinai, his face took on a glow because he had been with God.) Angels don't *have* to come shining brightly, but many of them do. Halos have become a popular way of showing that angels give off God's glory or brightness, but they don't give a very good picture of the glory and power that angels actually have.

KEY VERSES: *As I [Daniel] stood there, I looked up. And suddenly there stood before me a person dressed in linen clothes. He had a belt of purest gold around his waist. And his skin was glowing and lustrous! From his face came blinding flashes like lightning. And his eyes were pools of fire. His arms and feet shone like polished brass. His voice was like the roaring of a great crowd of people. (Daniel 10:5-6)*

RELATED VERSES: *Matthew 28:2-3; Luke 2:9; 24:4; 2 Thessalonians 1:7*

RELATED QUESTIONS: *Are angels' clothes shiny? Do angels wear clothes?*

Q: WHY CAN'T I SEE ANGELS?

116

A: The Bible tells of angels appearing to people. Why don't they appear to us today? It may seem unfair or strange that you can't see angels, but angels are spirits. They don't have bodies as we do. Angels appear with physical bodies only when God sends them to speak to people. The times when angels have appeared to people (at least the ones we know about for sure) have been quite rare—only during the Exodus, the time of the judges, the time of Elijah, the time of Jesus' birth, and the time of the forming of the early church. In other words, God doesn't show off his angels. He saves angelic appearances for times when people really need to see them. Angels can do their work without being seen.

KEY VERSE: *An Angel of the Lord came and spoke to Philip. The Angel said, "Go over to the road that runs from Jerusalem through the Gaza Desert. Be there around noon." (Acts 8:26)*

RELATED VERSES: *Psalm 34:7; Acts 10:22*

RELATED QUESTIONS: *Will God let us see an angel in these days? How come God wants it so you can't see the angels? How come angels disappear?*

NOTE TO PARENTS: *The real question here may be, If angels are real, why can't I see them? Explain to your child that there are a lot of things that are real that they can't see, such as electricity, oxygen, etc.*

Q: ARE THERE PEOPLE INSIDE OF ANGELS?

117

A: People and angels are two different kinds of beings altogether. There aren't any people inside angels, nor do people become angels when they die. In cartoons you may see people die and become angels, but that's not what really happens. People have souls. Our souls live forever as spiritual beings. In fact, here's a cool secret: When we get to heaven, we will get to rule the angels!

KEY VERSE: *Don't you know that we will judge the angels in Heaven? (1 Corinthians 6:3)*

RELATED VERSES: *Mark 12:25; Hebrews 2:5-8*

RELATED QUESTIONS: *How does a person become an angel? Were angels people before they died? Will we become angels when we get into heaven?*

Q: HOW MANY ANGELS ARE IN HEAVEN?

118

A: There's a huge number. We don't know how many angels are in heaven because the Bible doesn't give an exact number. But there are thousands and thousands—as many as God needs. Some people who have seen these large crowds of angels are Elisha and his servant, the shepherds at Christ's birth, and the apostle John.

___

KEY VERSE: *Then I [John] heard the singing of many angels. They were surrounding the throne and the Living Beings and the Elders. (Revelation 5:11)*

RELATED VERSES: *2 Kings 6:16-17; Luke 2:13; Hebrews 12:22; Revelation 7:9-11*

RELATED QUESTIONS: *How many angels are there? Does God have a sidekick angel? Does God have grandchildren in heaven?*

Q: HOW DID ANGELS GET THEIR WINGS?

119

A: Artists often paint angels as having wings, and people have written stories that describe angels as having wings or earning their wings. But the Bible doesn't say that all angels have wings. It does say that angels can fly and that, at times, they appear with wings. But angels don't need wings to fly, like birds or butterflies do. God made sure that they can get where they need to be when they need to be there.

KEY VERSE: *As I [Daniel] prayed, Gabriel flew swiftly to me. He is the angel I had seen in the earlier vision. (Daniel 9:21)*

RELATED VERSES: *Isaiah 6:1-2; Ezekiel 1:6-9, 23-24*

RELATED QUESTIONS: *Why do angels fly? Do angels look the same as the ones we make in the snow? Do angels really look like they do in pictures? Do all angels have wings? How come in pictures angels have wings? Do angels have wings, or do they just look like men in pajamas?*

Q: CAN ANGELS DIE?

120

A: If angels had bodies like people do, they would die, just like people do. But angels don't have bodies. They're spiritual beings, which means that they have no flesh or blood. Angels are spirits, invisible to us but still very real. Angels aren't born, either—they're created. Because angels don't have bodies, they can't grow old and die. But at the final judgment after the world ends, God will destroy Satan and the bad angels (see Revelation 20:11-14).

KEY VERSE: *[People] will never die again. In these ways they are like angels and are sons of God. For they are raised up in new life from the dead. (Luke 20:36)*

RELATED QUESTIONS: *If angels fight, can they get hurt? Do angels take care of themselves?*

Q: DO ANGELS GO TO WORK?

121

A: The word *angel* means "messenger." Angels don't have jobs where they work for pay, the way people do. Instead, they serve God. Angels do nothing but what God wants them to do all the time, without ever getting tired or grumpy. They're happy to do it. They do a lot of work, but they don't "go to work" like your mom or dad does.

KEY VERSE: *The angels are spirits who serve God. They are messengers sent to care for those who will receive [Christ's] salvation. (Hebrews 1:14)*

RELATED VERSES: *Luke 4:10; 16:22; Revelation 4:8; 7:15*

RELATED QUESTIONS: *What does my angel do? Can angels build things? Why does God use angels—why doesn't he do everything?*

Q: DO ANGELS WATCH TELEVISION?

122

A: Angels spend all their time doing what God wants them to do and praising him. They don't take time to relax or do things "just for fun." Keep in mind that angels don't need to relax, because they don't get tired. And they enjoy their service to God so much that stopping to do something else wouldn't be "fun" for them anyway. Why would angels want to watch the stuff on TV when they can see the stars up close, fly through the universe doing errands for God, and watch God doing miracles in people's lives? Angels have much better things to do than watch TV—they help us!

KEY VERSE: *These Living Beings . . . didn't rest day or night. They said, "Holy, holy, holy, Lord God Almighty! He was, and is, and is coming." (Revelation 4:8)*

RELATED VERSES: *Hebrews 1:14; Revelation 7:11-12*

RELATED QUESTIONS: *What do angels do all day long when they are not protecting people from getting kidnapped? Can angels get bored?*

Q: DOES EACH ANGEL BELONG TO A PERSON?

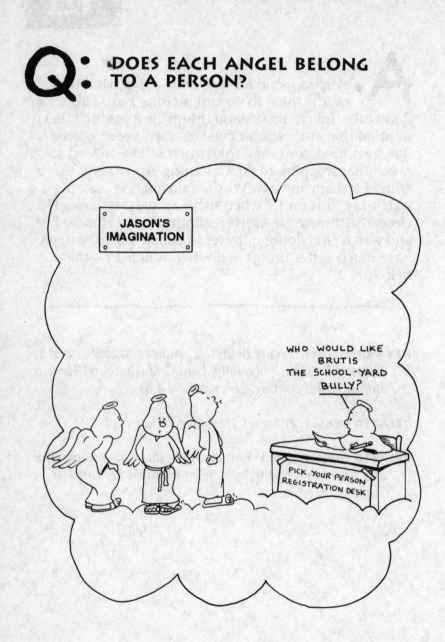

123

A: The Bible says that angels help people, but it doesn't say each angel watches over a certain person like a bodyguard. You may have heard people say that God assigns an angel to watch over each person, but we don't know whether that's true. We only know that God gives angels the job of helping and protecting us. We don't know how they divide that job.

KEY VERSE: *Be careful that you don't look down upon a single one of these children. For I [Jesus] tell you that in Heaven their angels can speak directly to my Father. (Matthew 18:10)*

RELATED VERSES: *Psalm 34:7; 91:11; Ezekiel 28:14; Hebrews 1:14*

RELATED QUESTIONS: *Does every person have a guardian angel? Do I have a guardian angel?*

NOTE TO PARENTS: *There is a Jewish tradition that angels look like the person to whom they are assigned.*

Q: ARE THERE ANGELS IN THIS ROOM WITH US?

124

A: Angels aren't everywhere, so we shouldn't expect them to be with us at every moment, the way God is. But angels *may* be in the room with you right now. Angels *can* be with us without our knowing about it. In the Bible story about Balaam (Numbers 22:21-41), Balaam didn't know there was an angel with him until God allowed him to see the angel. Angels are invisible spirits, so we never know exactly where they are.

KEY VERSE: *Don't forget to be kind to strangers. Some who have done this have served angels without knowing it! (Hebrews 13:2)*

RELATED VERSES: *Numbers 22:22-35; 2 Kings 6:16-17; Hebrews 1:14*

RELATED QUESTION: *Why are angels kept in heaven?*

Q: DO ANGELS STAY IN THE CAR OR FLY BESIDE?

125

A: God watches over us, using angels as his servants. If God wants an angel to be with you in the car, that is where the angel will be. If God wants the angel to be outside the car and moving along at sixty-five miles per hour, that's where the angel will be. Angels go wherever God tells them to go.

KEY VERSE: *Shall I look to the mountains for help? No! My help comes from the Lord. (Psalm 121:1-2)*

RELATED VERSE: *Matthew 28:20*

RELATED QUESTIONS: *Do angels protect us all the time? If angels are always around us, how come some people die?*

Q: DO ANGELS SIN?

126

A: We don't know if angels can sin anymore. Human beings sin because they have a desire to sin. That is because after Adam and Eve disobeyed God in the Garden of Eden, every person ever born has been born a sinner. Angels are not like human beings, and they don't have a desire to sin. So it is not natural for angels to disobey God.

The Bible hints that they may be able to do wrong. Satan was once an angel who was thrown out of heaven because he wanted to take God's place. And other angels sinned then by following Satan. But can other angels sin now? We don't know. We know only that heaven cannot have any sin in it; if it did, it would not be perfect.

KEY VERSE: *God cannot even trust his own messengers. Even angels make mistakes! (Job 4:18)*

RELATED VERSES: *Job 15:15; 2 Peter 2:4; Jude 1:6*

RELATED QUESTIONS: *Does God like it when people say to you, "Oh, you are a little angel"? Do angels do what they are supposed to do by themselves, or does God have to tell them what to do? How do angels know to obey God? If angels were bad once, can they still be bad?*

Q: CAN AN ANGEL BE YOUR FRIEND AND TELL YOU THAT HE IS YOUR ANGEL?

127

A: In the Bible, we learn that God wants to be good friends with people. He doesn't give that job to angels. God called Abraham his friend. God spoke to Moses in the way that a man would speak to a friend. That's what he wants with us, too. God's angels do his work, but they don't try to become friends with us because the one looking for our friendship is God. If God has given you an angel, you won't see that angel or talk to him.

KEY VERSE: *I [Jesus] no longer call you slaves. For a master doesn't confide in his slaves. Now you are my friends. This is proved by the fact that I have told you all that the Father told me. (John 15:15)*

RELATED VERSE: *Exodus 33:11*

RELATED QUESTIONS: *Can I talk to angels? Can you play with angels? Can you have a relationship with an angel?*

Q: DO ANGELS JUST APPEAR FOR AN INSTANT ONE MINUTE AND THEN DISAPPEAR?

128

A: Angels are not ghosts, gods, or superheroes. They serve God and always follow his directions, so they go wherever he says and appear however he tells them to. They appear to us the way they need to appear to do God's work. In the Bible we sometimes read of angels coming and going quickly, but they never did it to show off. In fact, usually no one saw them appear or disappear.

KEY VERSE: *Suddenly, the angel was joined by a great crowd of others. All the armies of Heaven were there! They were praising God. (Luke 2:13)*

RELATED VERSES: *Luke 2:8-15*

NOTE TO PARENTS: *Some children may ask this question because they think they may have seen an angel, and they want to know if it is possible. Others may ask this because of the way angels are pictured in movies and television shows. Emphasize the fact that the only reliable source for our information about angels is the Bible.*

Q: CAN AN ANGEL BE A PERSON TO US LIKE A REAL PERSON?

HERE YOU GO, ANGEL

129

A: Sometimes angels have made themselves look like humans and have appeared to people. That's how they appeared to Abraham one day. Abraham was sitting outside his tent when three men walked up and greeted him. As far as he knew, they were men, perhaps travelers looking for a place to stay. But in fact, they were angels. That's why the Bible urges us to be kind and neighborly to visitors. You never know when a visitor might be an angel. It is possible that you have met an angel and did not know it. But don't go looking for angels. Angels almost always stay invisible.

KEY VERSE: *Don't forget to be kind to strangers. Some who have done this have served angels without knowing it! (Hebrews 13:2)*

RELATED VERSES: *Genesis 18:1-2*

RELATED QUESTIONS: *Can we talk to our angels, to the ones who protect us? Does everyone have their own personal angel?*

Q: ARE DEMONS RED WITH HORNS AND LONG TAILS?

130

A: Sometimes cartoons and Halloween costumes show the devil and demons as red creatures with horns and long tails. But that idea of what Satan looks like came out of someone's imagination, not from the Bible. The devil is a bad angel, and angels don't have physical bodies, so no one knows what Satan looks like. Like other angels, the devil can take different forms if he wants to. But he's not a red-clothed lizard with a pitchfork. He's a real being, living in the spiritual realm.

Satan is God's enemy, but Satan is not as powerful as God. When Satan was created, he was good. But he later rebelled against God and was kicked out of heaven. Jesus called him "a liar and the father of lies." The Bible says he is an "angel of light." So we see that Satan can be very tricky—he tries to make bad look good. His main way of doing this is to lie to us and accuse us, not scare us with the way he looks.

KEY VERSE: *I remind you of the angels who were pure and holy. But they turned to a life of sin. Now God has them chained up in prisons of darkness. They are waiting for the Judgment Day. (Jude 1:6)*

RELATED VERSE: *1 Peter 5:8*

RELATED QUESTIONS: *Who is the devil? Can demons look like angels like Satan can? Did God actually kick the devil out of heaven?*

NOTE TO PARENTS: *Kids have the idea that the devil is God's equal, like a villain in a superhero cartoon. But the devil is no match for God. God is infinite and all-powerful, while Satan is a created being with limited power.*

Q:

WHY DID GOD MAKE SATAN IF GOD KNEW SATAN WOULD MAKE SIN?

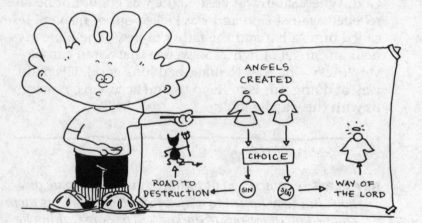

ANGELS CREATED

CHOICE

ROAD TO DESTRUCTION ← SIN

SIN → WAY OF THE LORD

131

A: God created all people and all angels with the ability to choose to obey him. God knew that some would choose to obey and some would choose to disobey. Still he created them because he knew it was a good thing to do. God makes everything good, and that includes the people and angels, who had the choice of whether or not to serve God. Also, Satan did not invent sin, but he tries to get people to choose it. God has allowed Satan to have freedom now, but in the end God will defeat Satan and punish him.

KEY VERSE: *I [Jesus] saw Satan falling from Heaven like a flash of light! (Luke 10:18)*

RELATED VERSES: *Revelation 20:7-10*

RELATED QUESTIONS: *If heaven was so perfect and Satan lived there before he sinned, why did he sin? Why didn't God stop Adam from eating the apple off the tree? Why did God make a bad tree in the Garden with Adam and Eve?*

Q: DOES THE DEVIL HAVE POWER LIKE GOD DOES?

RUMBLE RUMBLE

132

A: The devil has great powers, but he is not even close to being as powerful as God. Satan can perform fake miracles, lie, accuse, twist the truth, tempt, and trick people into doing what is wrong. But he also has many limits: He cannot be everywhere at the same time; he cannot create anything; he is not all-powerful; he cannot read your mind; and he has no power over Jesus.

KEY VERSES: *Dear friends, don't be afraid of these who want to murder you. They can only kill the body. They have no power over your souls. But I'll tell you whom to fear! Fear God who has the power to kill you and then put you into hell. (Luke 12:4-5)*

RELATED VERSES: *Job 1:6-12; 2:1-7; John 14:30*

RELATED QUESTIONS: *Is Satan as powerful as God? Does Satan ever get hurt? What is Satan's kingdom made up of? Why was Satan a snake when he tempted Eve?*

NOTE TO PARENTS: *You can assure your child that the devil has no power over Jesus (John 14:30). That's just one reason it's so great to be Jesus' friend.*

Q: WHAT MEAN THINGS DOES SATAN DO TO PEOPLE?

133

A: Satan does *not* get to do whatever he wants to do to people. The main thing he does is get us to hurt ourselves and others. Lots of people think that Satan only tempts people to do bad stuff. He does tempt us, but the worst thing he does is lie to us. Satan hates God and does not want us to believe what God says. He wants us to sin. He wants us to believe what is false. He wants us to believe that we are no good. Satan lies to us about our worth and about what really matters so we'll hurt ourselves. The way to see Satan's lies is to know the truth that's in the Bible, God's Word.

KEY VERSE: *Watch out for attacks from Satan, your great enemy. He prowls around like a hungry, roaring lion. He is always looking for someone to tear apart. (1 Peter 5:8)*

RELATED VERSES: *Genesis 3:1; Job 1:6-12; 2:1-7; Matthew 4:1; John 8:44; 14:30; 1 John 3:8; Revelation 12:9-10*

RELATED QUESTIONS: *Will I ever get a demon? Can people be demon possessed? Do demons live in some people's hearts?*

NOTE TO PARENTS: *Some children have heard of demon possession and wonder if it can happen to them. They may ask a question like this as a veiled way of asking the more frightening one. But the devil has no power over Jesus. If we have Jesus in our hearts, Satan won't be able to do whatever he wants to with us or make us do anything we don't want to do.*

Q: HOW COME THE DEVIL WANTS US TO BE BAD?

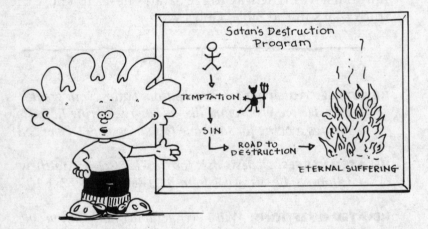

134

A: Satan's main purpose is to make us part of his kingdom, not just to make us bad. The devil would be quite happy if you lived a good life but never did anything for Jesus. He doesn't want you to serve God. He wants to hurt your faith in God, to make you doubt God's love and goodness. One of the ways he does that is to tempt you to do bad things. If Satan had his way, Christians would just sit around, doing nothing good and telling no one about Jesus.

KEY VERSE: *Then [false teachers] will come to their senses and escape from Satan's trap. He uses it to catch them whenever he likes. Then they can begin doing the will of God. (2 Timothy 2:26)*

RELATED VERSES: *John 17:15; 1 Peter 5:8-9*

RELATED QUESTIONS: *Why is the devil after us? Why was Satan so wicked? Why did Satan become so mean? Why is Satan so jealous? Why did Lucifer become bad?*

NOTE TO PARENTS: *Satan's main job is to lie to people, to get non-Christians to stay away from God, and to prevent Christians from serving God. He plants doubts and tries to convince us that we're not God's children.*

Q: ARE SATAN AND JESUS STILL AT WAR?

135

A: Jesus and Satan are definitely enemies at war, but Jesus will win. (By the way, when Jesus says to love your enemies, he's not talking about loving the devil. He's talking about loving people.) The devil will do everything in his power to try to stop people from believing in Jesus and living for Jesus. But we don't have to be afraid of Satan because God protects his people against Satan's power. Jesus never loses.

KEY VERSES: *Put on all of God's armor. Then you will be safe from Satan's attacks. We are not fighting against people made of flesh and blood. We are fighting against persons without bodies. They are the evil rulers of the unseen world. They are the satanic beings and evil princes of darkness who rule this world. They are the huge numbers of wicked spirits in the spirit world. (Ephesians 6:11-12)*

RELATED VERSES: *Hebrews 2:14; 1 John 2:14; Revelation 2:11; 12:7*

RELATED QUESTIONS: *Does Satan ever talk to God? Does God know the devil? Why does Satan want to be stronger than God? What does Jesus do all day? Does Jesus have a job in heaven? Does Jesus sleep?*

Q: WILL GOD FORGIVE SATAN?

136

A: God will never forgive Satan because Satan hates God and doesn't want to be forgiven. He doesn't want to have a relationship with God or to live in God's presence. He wants to take God's place. But God has already told us what will happen to Satan—he will be punished by being thrown in the lake of fire (hell), where he will suffer forever for his rebellion.

KEY VERSE: *Then the devil who tricked them will be thrown into the Lake of Fire. It is burning with sulfur where the Creature and False Prophet are. They will be tormented day and night forever and ever. (Revelation 20:10)*

RELATED VERSES: *Revelation 20:7-10*

RELATED QUESTIONS: *Can Satan turn back and become good? Why doesn't God kill Satan? If Satan knows that he isn't going to win against God, why doesn't he just become good again? Why did Satan start doing wicked things if he was an angel? Does God still love Satan, even when he does bad things to people?*

NOTE TO PARENTS: *Many people confuse niceness with God's love. They think that a loving God should be nice to everyone, even Satan. But a loving God does not love evil.*

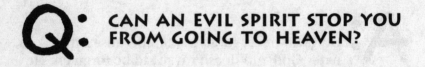

Q: CAN AN EVIL SPIRIT STOP YOU FROM GOING TO HEAVEN?

A: If a person has given his or her life to Christ, nothing can stop that person from going to heaven. The only thing the devil can do is invent lies that sound like truth and then hope people believe them. Satan can't send you to hell or keep you from going to heaven, no matter what he does.

KEY VERSES: *I am sure that nothing can ever separate us from [Christ's] love. Death can't, and life can't. The angels won't. All the powers of hell can't keep God's love away. . . . It doesn't matter if we are high above the sky, or deep in the ocean. Nothing can carry us away from God's love that is in our Lord Jesus Christ. (Romans 8:38-39)*

RELATED VERSES: *John 14:30; Philippians 1:6*

RELATED QUESTIONS: *Who goes to hell? Are there kids in hell? Can Christians go to hell? How do evil spirits come into you?*

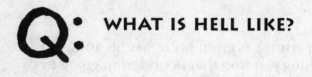

Q: WHAT IS HELL LIKE?

138

A: According to the Bible, hell is very dark and very painful. It is a place of eternal suffering and separation from God. It is a place of grim loneliness. The worst thing about hell is that it is separate from God and from all that is good. There is no love, joy, fun, laughter, or celebration in hell. Some people make jokes about hell and say that they want to go there to be with their friends. But no one will have any friends in hell. No one should want to go there.

KEY VERSE: *But [the rich man's] soul went into hell. There, in torment, he saw Lazarus far away with Abraham. (Luke 16:23)*

RELATED VERSES: *Matthew 5:22; 8:12; 25:41, 46; 2 Thessalonians 1:9; 2 Peter 2:4; Revelation 9:1-2, 11; 14:10-11; 20:10*

RELATED QUESTIONS: *Why is there hell? Where is hell? Is there fire in hell? Why is hell dark if they have fires? Is it hot in hell? Was there a fire when the devil went down to hell?*

NOTE TO PARENTS: *Be very serious when you explain hell to your children. At the same time, however, tell them about heaven, a place of eternal love, joy, fun, laughter, and celebration. And assure them that they can go to heaven if they trust in Jesus.*

Q: WHY DID AN ANGEL COME TO MARY?

139

A: An angel came to Mary to tell her God's message—God wanted Mary to know that she would be the mother of Jesus, God's Son. When Mary heard the news, she was frightened, but she was also very happy. More than anything, she wanted to obey God. And she felt very honored to be Jesus' mother.

KEY VERSE: *God sent the angel Gabriel to Nazareth. (Luke 1:26)*

RELATED VERSES: *Luke 1:26-38*

RELATED QUESTIONS: *What was the name of the angel who came to Mary? What angel came to tell the shepherds about Jesus' birth?*

NOTE TO PARENTS: *This is a good time to let your children know that God is able to show them his plan for their lives. God's plan probably won't be announced by an angel, but God will tell it to them when they seek him.*

Q: WHY WAS THERE AN ANGEL AND A FIERY SWORD GUARDING THE ENTRANCE TO THE GARDEN OF EDEN?

140

A: An angel stood at the entrance to the Garden of Eden to keep Adam and Eve from going back in. God had sent them out of the Garden because they had sinned. Because they disobeyed God, they would never be allowed to live in Eden again.

KEY VERSE: *God expelled [Adam]. And God placed mighty angels at the east of the Garden of Eden. They stood with a flaming sword to guard the entrance to the Tree of Life. (Genesis 3:24)*

RELATED VERSES: *Numbers 22:31; 1 Chronicles 21:27-30; Luke 4:10*

RELATED QUESTIONS: *How did Satan disguise himself as a snake? Did the serpent bite? When you're in heaven, can you still see the angel that is guarding the entrance to Eden? Did Adam and Eve go to heaven when they died?*

Q: WHO WAS THE ANGEL OF THE LORD?

141

A: The Bible mentions the angel of the Lord many times. In the desert, when Moses saw the bush that was burning but wasn't burning up, it was the angel of the Lord who spoke to him out of it. Who was this who spoke? Some people think it was a special appearance of God and not actually an angel. But usually the phrase "angel of the Lord" is just a good way to describe an angel. It probably does not refer to one specific angel.

KEY VERSE: *The Angel of the Lord came to [Gideon]. He said, "Mighty soldier, the Lord is with you!" (Judges 6:12)*

RELATED VERSES: *Exodus 3:2; Numbers 22:22; 2 Samuel 24:16; 1 Chronicles 21:16*

RELATED QUESTION: *Why do people call an angel "angel of the Lord"?*

NOTE TO PARENTS: *It is important to help your child focus on God, not on angels. The message sender and the message are most important, not the messengers.*

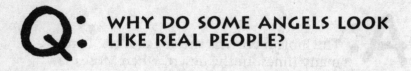

Q: WHY DO SOME ANGELS LOOK LIKE REAL PEOPLE?

142

A: The word *angel* means "messenger," and God sometimes sends these messengers to take messages to people. The Bible describes them as bringing these messages while in the form of human beings. God can send angels to encourage a person, comfort someone, or merely to deliver news. If angels always appeared as blazing towers of fire, they would scare people away. Sometimes God wants angels to frighten people. But at other times he wants his messengers to hide their true identity as angels for a while; then they appear as people.

KEY VERSE: *All at once [Abraham] saw three men coming toward him. He jumped up and ran to meet them and welcomed them. (Genesis 18:2)*

RELATED VERSES: *Genesis 19:1; Judges 6:11-12; 13:15-18; Daniel 9:21; Acts 12:7; Hebrews 1:14*

RELATED QUESTION: *Can angels be here with us?*

Q: WHY DO SOME ANGELS HAVE FOUR FACES?

VIDEO MONITOR

OFF ON
CONTROL SWITCH

My Angel

143

A: When the Bible describes angels as having four faces, it is not giving us a picture of what angels actually look like (like a photograph). Remember, angels don't have physical bodies, so they don't have faces the way people do. When a prophet saw an angel with four faces, God was telling him that angels have many abilities—that angels show us several things about God, that they can see in any direction, and that they can serve God in any way needed at any time.

KEY VERSE: *Each of the four Guardian Angels had four faces. The first was that of an ox. The second was a man's face. The third was a lion's face. And the fourth was an eagle's face. (Ezekiel 10:14)*

RELATED VERSES: *Ezekiel 10:1-22*

Q: WHY DIDN'T AN ANGEL TAKE JESUS OFF THE CROSS?

144

A: It was God's will for Jesus to die on the cross. Jesus could have called on thousands of angels to rescue him, but he did not do that because he was dying for us, taking the punishment for our sins. If angels had stepped in and rescued Jesus, he would not have died, and then we would not be forgiven. Jesus' disciple Peter tried to stop Jesus from being arrested, but Jesus told him not to do that because it was God's plan for him to die.

Just before Jesus died, he cried out, "My God, my God, why have you forsaken me?" meaning that God had left him totally alone. No one was there to help him or comfort him, not even the angels. This was part of his suffering for our sins.

KEY VERSES: *Don't you know that I [Jesus] could call on my Father? He could send thousands of angels to keep us safe! And he could send them right away! But if I did this, how would the Scriptures be fulfilled? For they foretold what is happening now. (Matthew 26:53-54)*

RELATED VERSES: *Matthew 26:51-54; Mark 8:31; 15:34-37*

RELATED QUESTIONS: *Where were the angels when Jesus died? Why didn't an angel take Jesus' crown off of him? Why did an angel come to the tomb after Jesus had left?*

Q: WHICH ANGEL IS BEST AFTER GOD AND THEN JESUS?

145

A: The Bible uses the word *archangel* to describe one type of angel that seems to be more important than regular angels. Only Michael is said to be an archangel, but we don't know if he is the only one. The Bible also refers to princes among the angels. That seems to suggest that some angels are more powerful than others. Angels are not equal to Jesus, though. They aren't gods, nor are they God's buddies. Angels are created beings who obey and worship God.

KEY VERSE: *For 21 days the Evil Spirit who rules the kingdom of Persia blocked my [the angel's] way. Then Michael, one of the top officers of the heavenly army, came to help me. So I was able to get past these spirit rulers of Persia. (Daniel 10:13)*

RELATED VERSES: *Daniel 10:21; 1 Thessalonians 4:16; Hebrews 1:3-13; 2:5-8; Jude 1:9*

RELATED QUESTION: *Does God have a bodyguard?*

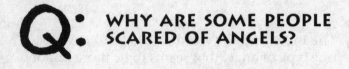

Q: WHY ARE SOME PEOPLE SCARED OF ANGELS?

146

A: In the Bible, we read that some people became frightened when angels appeared to them. They were scared because they were amazed at the power and glory of the angels. God is great and holy and awesome, and sometimes angels appear with a lot of light and noise. That can be quite scary. Also, remember that most people have never seen an angel. So when one appears, it is quite normal to be surprised and fearful. Many times when angels appeared, they had to tell the people they visited not to be afraid. God sends angels to us to help us, so we don't need to be afraid of them.

KEY VERSE: *Then the Angel touched the meat and bread with his staff. Fire flamed up from the rock and burned them up! And suddenly the Angel was gone! (Judges 6:21)*

RELATED VERSES: *1 Chronicles 21:30; Matthew 28:2-4; Luke 1:13, 28-30; 2:9-10; Revelation 22:8-9*

Q: WHY DID GOD MAKE HEAVEN?

147

A: God has only one use for heaven, and that is to share it with us. God is everywhere. When we talk about heaven, we are really talking about where God lives. We think of heaven as a place because that's how we describe going to be with God. But remember, God isn't just in one place—he's everywhere!

In the Bible, the word *heaven* can refer to several places: (1) the home or place of God; (2) the new Jerusalem; or (3) "the heavens," or sky. Just before Jesus left the earth, he said he would go and prepare a place for us, a place where we can live with him. Someday he will come back and set it all up for us—he will destroy this world and create a new one. That new world will be for all those who love him. That's the heaven that God will make for all believers to live in forever.

KEY VERSES: *There are many homes in my Father's house. I am going to prepare a place for you. I will come again and take you to me. Then you will be with me where I am about to go. If this weren't so, I would tell you plainly. (John 14:2-3)*

RELATED VERSES: *Hebrews 9:24; Revelation 21:3*

RELATED QUESTIONS: *What is heaven? What is heaven like? Why did God come to the earth? Is hell near heaven?*

NOTE TO PARENTS: *Heaven is one of the Christian's great hopes. It is God's guarantee that the evil, injustice, and cruelty of life here on earth will end and be put right. People without hope in Christ can feel overwhelmed by fear of the future, but Christians need not be afraid. Share this hope with your child.*

Q: IS JESUS THE ONLY WAY TO HEAVEN?

148

A: Yes, Jesus is the only way to heaven. He said, "No one can get to the Father except through me." Just as the only right answer to 2 + 2 is 4, Jesus is the only answer to our need for forgiveness. He is the only one who has the right to take away our sins, since he died for us. He is the only one who has the power to take them away, since he is God. And he is the only one who can be perfectly fair to every single person, from babies never born to the most wicked person who ever lived, since he is just and merciful. Since Jesus has offered a clear way to heaven, why would anyone look for any other way?

KEY VERSE: *Jesus said, "I am the Way, the Truth, and the Life. No one can get to the Father except through me." (John 14:6)*

RELATED VERSES: *John 6:68; Revelation 22:17*

RELATED QUESTIONS: *Why is heaven the only way? If you believe in God but you never asked Jesus as your Lord and Savior, can you still go to heaven? If babies die before they are born, do they go to heaven?*

NOTE TO PARENTS: *A question like this usually means that other children were discussing their beliefs with your child. Take this time to reassure your child that belief in Christ is the only way to heaven, and take some time to pray with your child for his or her friends.*

Q: ARE ALL PEOPLE NICE IN HEAVEN?

149

A: All the people in heaven are nice because everyone there loves God and loves one another. No one will hurt anyone or be mean to anyone in heaven. There will be no crying or pain. There will be no pushing or shoving or name-calling in heaven. The Bible says that in heaven we will know God like he knows us. When we know and understand God and his love, we won't want to hurt anyone ever again.

_____

KEY VERSE: *Don't you know that those doing such [evil] things can't share in God's Kingdom? (1 Corinthians 6:9)*

RELATED VERSES: *Revelation 21:4, 8; 22:14-15*

RELATED QUESTIONS: *Will bullies call me names in heaven? What if someone bad tricks Jesus and sneaks into heaven and hits people?*

NOTE TO PARENTS: *Be careful not to give the impression that being nice gets you into heaven. While all people of God should be kind, not all kind people are people of God. Also, the question behind the question here may involve fear of others—the child wants assurance that in heaven no one will hurt him or her. You can assure your child that there are no bullies in heaven. Heaven is the safest, most wonderful place ever made.*

Q: CAN YOU FALL OUT OF HEAVEN?

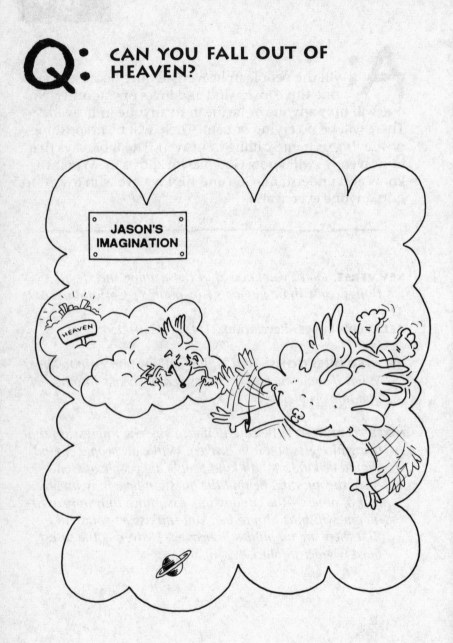

JASON'S IMAGINATION

HEAVEN

150

A: People cannot fall out of heaven any more than they can fall out of their own front yard. You may have seen pictures or cartoons that show heaven as a place up in the sky or in the clouds. We don't know where heaven is; we only know that God and Jesus are there. Someday God will make a new earth and a new city called the new Jerusalem, where all his people will live forever. That place will be perfect for us—no dangerous streets, no diseases to catch, nothing to worry about at all. In heaven, you will never hear anyone say, "Be careful!" because you won't have any dangers to be careful about.

KEY VERSE: *I heard a loud shout from the throne. It was saying, "Look, the home of God is now among men. He will live with them and they will be his people. Yes, God himself will be among them." (Revelation 21:3)*

RELATED VERSES: *Romans 8:39; Revelation 22:14*

RELATED QUESTIONS: *Are there police in heaven? Will there be any doors in heaven? Does heaven move?*

NOTE TO PARENTS: *This question comes up when children confuse heaven with a physical location, usually one that is up in the sky. They are not able to imagine a spiritual—as opposed to physical—reality, so they can't imagine heaven not being a place. They naturally think of heaven as being up because that's where we put it in our descriptions of it.*

Q: IS HEAVEN ALL MADE UP OF CLOUDS?

JASON'S
IMAGINATION

151

A: Sometimes cartoons and movies show funny pictures of angels standing in clouds. But heaven is not made up of clouds. The Bible does say that clouds surround God's throne, that Jesus was caught up in the clouds, and that when Jesus returns he will come in the clouds. But those are word pictures. They don't mean that heaven is made up of rain clouds. Heaven is God's presence. It's a spiritual place. It's a world invisible to us now but very real just the same.

KEY VERSE: *Then the scene changed. I saw a white cloud. Someone was sitting on it, and he looked like Jesus. He was called "The Son of Man." He had a crown of gold on his head and a sickle in his hand. (Revelation 14:14)*

RELATED VERSES: *Psalm 97:2; Luke 21:27; 1 Thessalonians 4:17*

RELATED QUESTIONS: *Is there going to be summer and fall in heaven? Will there be any winter? Will our house be warm? Does it rain in heaven? Can you walk on clouds in heaven? Are there bathrooms in heaven? Is there water in heaven?*

NOTE TO PARENTS: *Children pick up a lot of wrong ideas about heaven from cartoons and other popular tales. If you're not sure how to explain what's wrong with a false idea, it's better to say "I don't know how to explain it" than to fall back on a popular fantasy. Sit down with them and read Revelation 21–22 together so they can see what the Bible says about heaven and the new Jerusalem.*

Q: WHY IS HEAVEN SO SHINY?

152

A: Heaven shines with the brightness of the glory of God. God is perfect, holy, 100 percent good. Because of that, God shines with light. Many descriptions of heaven mention light and gold because of God's glory.

KEY VERSE: *Great bursts of light flashed forth from him. It was like light from a glittering diamond or from a shining ruby. There was a rainbow glowing like an emerald around his throne. (Revelation 4:3)*

RELATED VERSES: *Revelation 4:1-6; 21:18-21, 23; 22:5*

RELATED QUESTIONS: *Will there be night in heaven? Why does God stay up all night? What does my mansion in heaven look like?*

Q: ARE THE STREETS IN HEAVEN REAL GOLD OR JUST PAINTED WITH GOLD?

153

A: All of heaven is real—none of it is fake. When we get there, it will be the most real, beautiful place we have ever seen. Will even the gold be real? The Bible says that the streets will be paved with gold. This may just be a way of saying that it's a great place to be, like saying "It must be a million degrees out here" to describe a really hot day. Or it may refer to real gold streets running through town. It's hard to know *exactly* what heaven will be like because we really can't understand it now.

Imagine a frog trying to explain life on land to a tadpole. All the descriptions would sound bad—you can't swim, there's no water, etc. The frog can't really tell the tadpole what life on land is like. Only when the tadpole becomes a frog can the tadpole understand. Only when we get to heaven will we know what it will be like. But one thing is for sure: Nothing will be fake!

KEY VERSE: *The 12 gates were made of pearls. Each gate was made from a single pearl! And the main street was pure, clear gold, like glass. (Revelation 21:21)*

RELATED VERSES: *Revelation 21:1–22:21*

RELATED QUESTIONS: *What will God's house be made of? What will God's house look like in heaven? Is heaven more beautiful than the most beautiful place on earth? What is heaven made of? How does God make things out of gold? Does God use glue to make gold stick to the new Jerusalem? Are the gates in heaven made out of gold?*

Q: DOES GOD HAVE ANGELS WATCHING OVER HEAVEN SO DEMONS CAN'T GET IN?

154

A: God will let no evil at all into heaven—no sin, no hurting, no demons. Life in heaven will be *safe*. In fact, heaven is the safest place anywhere—perfectly safe all the time. No one in heaven is afraid of anything, and no one there ever gets hurt.

KEY VERSE: *[God] will swallow up death forever. The Lord God will wipe away all tears. He will take away all insults and mockery against his land and people forever. The Lord has spoken! He will surely do it! (Isaiah 25:8)*

RELATED VERSES: *Revelation 7:17; 22:3-5*

RELATED QUESTIONS: *Is heaven a safe place? Will I be safe in heaven? Does God keep bad stuff out of heaven? Can the devil still hurt you when you're in heaven? Will snakes be there? Will we be able to see Satan in heaven?*

NOTE TO PARENTS: *Every child craves safety and fears danger. A safe place is a happy place, and conversely, a dangerous place isn't. In order to be happy, a child needs to feel safe. A question like this one, therefore, applies a child's test of happiness to heaven: If it isn't safe, then it can't be happy. You can reassure your child that no place is safer than heaven.*

Q: WHERE DID GOD LIVE BEFORE HEAVEN WAS MADE?

155

A: God has always lived in heaven because heaven is the place where God is. God has made a place for us where he is—so that is heaven for us. Wherever God is, there is heaven.

KEY VERSE: *Our Father in Heaven, we honor your holy name. (Matthew 6:9)*

RELATED VERSES: *Deuteronomy 26:15; 1 Kings 8:30, 39, 43, 49*

RELATED QUESTIONS: *Where does God live? How does God get down here (to live in us)—does he fly? How can God be in more than one place at one time? How long did it take to make heaven?*

NOTE TO PARENTS: *Sometimes a child's question comes from a faulty assumption about God. You can use questions like this to explain how God is different from us.*

Q: DOES JESUS LIVE WITH GOD IN HEAVEN, OR DOES HE LIVE BY HIMSELF?

156

A: When Jesus left the earth, he went to heaven to live with God the Father. That's where he is right now. He sits at the Father's right hand, the place of highest honor. The Bible says he talks to God about us (1 John 2:1).

KEY VERSE: *Now I am leaving the world, and leaving them behind. And I am coming to you. Holy Father, keep them in your own care. Keep all those you have given me. May they be united just as we are. (John 17:11)*

RELATED VERSES: *John 17:5; Acts 7:55-56; Romans 8:34; Colossians 3:1; Hebrews 10:12*

RELATED QUESTIONS: *Will Jesus do miracles in heaven? Is Jesus happy in heaven? When God is in heaven, is he always thinking of people down here on earth? Does God take care of his angels the way he takes care of his people? Is God like the president of the United States in heaven?*

Q: WHY DOESN'T GOD TAKE US TO HEAVEN AS SOON AS WE GET SAVED?

SEE, THIS IS WHAT JESUS DID FOR US.

JESUS

157

A: God doesn't take his people to heaven right away because he wants them to grow in their faith. He also wants them to tell others about Christ, to help others, and to make the world better. God has work for his people to do.

KEY VERSES: *So now go and make disciples in all the nations. Baptize them into the name of the Father, the Son, and the Holy Spirit. Then teach these new disciples to obey all the commands I have given you. (Matthew 28:19-20)*

RELATED VERSES: *John 9:4; 2 Peter 3:9*

Q: WHAT IF I DON'T WANT TO LEAVE MY FRIENDS AND FAMILY TO GO TO HEAVEN?

158

A: It's OK to not want to go to heaven right now. God has given you a place to enjoy right here and now—your home and your family and friends. You don't have to go to heaven right away.

But heaven will be a happy place, not a lonely or a sad place. Once you're in heaven you won't feel afraid of it—you will be glad that you are there. And if your family and friends know Jesus, too, you all will be in heaven together. You will be together with your family again.

KEY VERSE: *Be sure of this thing! I am with you always, even to the end of the world. (Matthew 28:20)*

RELATED VERSES: *Revelation 21:3-5*

RELATED QUESTIONS: *Will I be able to play with my friends up in heaven? How can you get out of heaven? What will my friend do when he goes to heaven? Do they have sports in heaven?*

NOTE TO PARENTS: *Don't be appalled if your child says he or she is afraid of heaven or doesn't want to go. Some kids fear going to heaven because it seems faraway and mysterious. All they can imagine is being taken away from their families and going to a cold and impersonal place where they don't know anyone. Assure your child that heaven is a warm and happy place.*

Q: HOW LONG DOES IT TAKE TO GET TO HEAVEN FROM HERE?

159

A: It happens in an instant. It's like opening your eyes—you're suddenly there. That's because heaven isn't a faraway place but is the place where God is. He just takes you there. The Bible says that when Jesus comes back, he will change us "in the twinkling of an eye."

KEY VERSE: *It will all happen in a moment, in the twinkling of an eye. (1 Corinthians 15:52)*

RELATED VERSES: *2 Corinthians 5:6-8; Philippians 1:21-23; 1 Thessalonians 4:13-17*

RELATED QUESTIONS: *Is heaven far out in space? Where is heaven? Can birds just fly into heaven anytime they want to? If we went high enough into the sky, would we find heaven? Why can't we go to heaven and just see it and then come back? When you die, are you just dead for a few seconds and then you're in heaven?*

Q: DOES GOD PUT DOWN A LADDER TO BRING US TO HEAVEN?

JASON'S
IMAGINATION

160

A: God takes us to heaven as soon as we die— immediately. God doesn't need a ladder or an airplane or anything else; we will just be there with him. The Bible says that Jesus is preparing a place for us. Through faith in him, we can have forgiveness of sins. Then, when it comes time for God to take us to heaven, he will do it—he will take us to live with him in his home forever.

KEY VERSE: *The Lord himself will come down from Heaven. This will happen with a mighty shout. There will be the voice of the archangel and a trumpet of God. The believers who are dead will be the first to rise to meet the Lord. (1 Thessalonians 4:16)*

RELATED VERSES: *Luke 16:22-31; John 14:6*

RELATED QUESTIONS: *Do angels take people's souls up to heaven? Will Jesus help me fly up? How will Jesus get me there? How do we get to heaven? How does God get people to heaven? Does God put down a ladder so that when people die they just climb up it into heaven? Do angels carry me to heaven? Does God take us to heaven? Does Jesus come for you with his body?*

NOTE TO PARENTS: *This question can mean two things: (1) What method does God use to transport us to heaven? and (2) How can a person be forgiven and go to heaven? Make sure you know which question your child means. In Jesus' story about the rich man and Lazarus (Luke 16:22), he mentioned that the angels carried Lazarus to heaven. Angels may be involved in the process.*

Q: WHY DO PEOPLE DIE?

161

A: People die because of sin. When God created the first human beings, they weren't supposed to die. They would never grow old or wear out. But then they disobeyed God, and sin and death entered the world. From that point on, every person born has been born a sinner into a sinful world. With sin came death, and so plants, animals, and people started to die. *Every* person has to die. But people can live eternally, in heaven with God, if they trust in Christ and ask God to forgive their sins. In heaven we aren't broken anymore. There is no sickness or pain or dying there.

KEY VERSES: *You may eat any fruit in the garden except fruit from the Tree of Conscience. You must not eat from that tree. For its fruit will open your eyes. It will make you aware of right and wrong, good and bad. If you eat its fruit, you will be doomed to die. (Genesis 2:16-17)*

RELATED VERSES: *Romans 6:23; 1 Corinthians 15:22; Hebrews 9:27; James 1:15*

RELATED QUESTIONS: *What is death? Why do I have to die? Why do some people die when they're young and not just when they're old? If God wants everyone to live, why do babies die? Do you grow older when you go to heaven?*

NOTE TO PARENTS: *This question often comes up when a relative or a pet dies. It is a good question and an important one for you to answer because it creates a "teachable moment." Answering it will probably lead to several more questions about salvation, eternal life, and heaven, so be prepared!*

Q: DOES YOUR BODY STAY IN THE GRAVE WHEN YOU GO TO HEAVEN?

162

A: The body you have here on earth is a physical, imperfect, short-term holding place for your soul. It's not made to last. When it's dead, it will decay. The real you is your soul, not your body. But in heaven you will be given a new body, a body that will last forever. This is known as the resurrection. The physical body will die, but the spiritual body will last forever. What happens to your body on earth or in the grave will not affect your eternal life in any way.

KEY VERSE: *For you [God] will not leave me among the dead. You will not let your loved one rot in the grave. (Psalm 16:10)*

RELATED VERSES: *Psalm 49:15; 1 Corinthians 15:35, 42-44*

RELATED QUESTIONS: *Will we be able to breathe in heaven? Does your spirit have clothes on when it leaves your body, or is it naked? What does it feel like when your spirit leaves your body? When you die are you automatically in heaven?*

Q: WILL I GO TO HEAVEN WHEN I DIE?

163

A: Every person who trusts in Jesus gets to go to heaven. If you have asked Jesus to take away your sins, then you will go to heaven, too. That's God's promise. And nothing can take away God's promise of heaven. When you die as a Christian, you go straight to live with God—you don't need to be afraid of dying.

KEY VERSE: *It is God's will that I should not lose even one of all those he has given me. It is his will that I should raise them to eternal life at the Last Day. (John 6:39)*

RELATED VERSES: *Isaiah 12:2; Romans 8:38-39; Hebrews 2:14; 6:11; 10:19-22; 2 Peter 1:10-11; 1 John 5:13*

RELATED QUESTIONS: *What if I die when I'm six or seven or eight? When will I die? When will we be dead? When I die, will I go straight to heaven?*

NOTE TO PARENTS: *Many children have a profound fear of death. They may have nightmares about it. But they may also hesitate to talk about it with you, so you may not hear them ask about it. Reassure them: Jesus defeated death. He made it possible for us to live forever in heaven. We don't need to fear death.*

Q: IS THERE ANY OTHER PLACE YOU CAN GO TO BESIDES HEAVEN OR HELL WHEN YOU DIE?

164

A: You may have heard people talk about purgatory, limbo, or some other in-between place where people go after they die. But the Bible does not teach anything about a place like that. The Bible does teach, however, that death is the final cutoff point. People do not have a second chance after they die. There is no opportunity after death to undo the bad things a person did while alive. The Bible also makes it very clear that Christians immediately go to be with God after they die.

KEY VERSE: *Jesus replied, "Today you will be with me in Paradise. This is a solemn promise." (Luke 23:43)*

RELATED VERSES: *Psalm 86:13; Proverbs 1:12; Luke 23:40-43; Hebrews 9:27*

RELATED QUESTION: *Does your soul stay in your body until you are buried or just until you die?*

Q: CAN GOD TAKE YOU TO HEAVEN IF YOU'RE NOT DEAD YET?

165

A: God can do anything. He can take a person to heaven anytime he likes, even if that person has not died. And in fact, the Bible tells about two people who had that privilege: Enoch and Elijah. God took them directly to heaven before they died. The Bible also tells us that someday Jesus will come back and take all his people to heaven, even those who have not died yet.

KEY VERSE: *When [Enoch] was 365, he disappeared. God took him away! (Genesis 5:24)*

RELATED VERSES: *2 Kings 2:11-12; 1 Corinthians 15:51; 1 Thessalonians 4:15-17*

RELATED QUESTIONS: *Why did Elijah get taken into heaven by a whirlwind when he hadn't died yet? Will we go to heaven in a fiery chariot?*

166

A: Death is a scary thing because it is final. After a person dies, that person does not come back to earth ever again. It's not like going on a trip and then coming back. It's like going on a trip and *never* coming back.

Death also scares us because it can happen so suddenly. One second the person is here, awake and talking. Then he or she is dead, unable to talk or live with us ever again.

That's why cemeteries are so creepy. No one wants to die, and cemeteries are where dead bodies are buried. Also, television and movies show cemeteries as places where ghosts and other spooky things hang out. Because most people fear death, a cemetery can be a scary place. But Christians don't have to be afraid of death because they know that they will go to heaven when they die and that scary things are just made up by people who make movies and TV shows.

KEY VERSES: *Even now, just as in the past, I hope that I will be an honor to Christ. This is true whether I live or die. For to me, living is Christ, and dying—well, that's better yet! (Philippians 1:20-21)*

RELATED VERSES: *Proverbs 10:24; Luke 8:49-56; Romans 8:38-39; 1 Corinthians 3:22*

RELATED QUESTIONS: *Why is everybody buried together in a cemetery instead of by themselves? How can they make room in the cemetery for everyone who is dead?*

NOTE TO PARENTS: *Help your children develop a healthy attitude about death. Say positive things as you pass a cemetery; don't jokingly say things that foster a fear of death.*

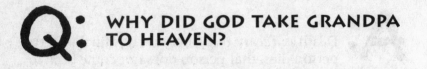

Q: WHY DID GOD TAKE GRANDPA TO HEAVEN?

167

A: We don't like to think about this fact, but it is true—eventually every person has to die. Sometimes people die when they are young, through accidents, diseases, or other tragedies. But even the healthiest person will die someday. As we get older, our bodies get weaker and weaker and then finally wear out.

No one wants a grandfather or grandmother to die, but that's part of God's plan right now: We get old and our bodies die. Certainly it is better to be with God in heaven than to be on earth. If our grandparents believe in Jesus, then someday we will see them again.

KEY VERSE: *[God's] loved ones are very special to him. He does not lightly let them die. (Psalm 116:15)*

RELATED VERSES: *Proverbs 16:31; 20:29*

RELATED QUESTIONS: *When I go up to heaven will I see my grandma? Will God let me visit Grandpa in heaven? If a whole family dies on earth, like in a fire, will they be together in a house in heaven?*

Q: HOW CAN JESUS RESURRECT BODIES THAT HAVE BEEN BURNT TO ASHES?

168

A: God will have no trouble finding everyone's molecules. He created people in the first place, so why wouldn't he be able to put them back together? It doesn't matter what happens to a person's body—God can put anyone back together. Whether the person's body was burned, separated for organ donations, or decayed in the ground, God will make it new and immortal. The earth and sea will give up their dead, and God will resurrect us despite the fact that we "returned to dust."

KEY VERSES: *When Jesus comes back, God will bring back with him all the dead Christians. . . . The believers who are dead will be the first to rise to meet the Lord. Then we who are alive and remain on the earth will be caught up with them. We will go to the clouds to meet the Lord in the air. We will stay with him forever. (1 Thessalonians 4:14, 16-17)*

RELATED VERSES: *Psalm 90:3; Ecclesiastes 3:20; Revelation 20:12-13*

RELATED QUESTIONS: *How can Jesus resurrect your body if it's turned to compost? If people have been dead for a long time, do they turn to compost? If someone hurts you really bad, like a bad person cuts off your head, and God really loves you, will he give you a new body? Isn't it gross to have worms chewing your body after you're dead?*

Q: WHY DO PEOPLE BELIEVE IN REINCARNATION?

169

A: Reincarnation is the belief that people come back to life after they die. They never really die once and for all but keep coming back as something else or as someone else. This belief says that people come back to earth as different creatures after they die.

Some people believe in reincarnation because their religion, such as Hinduism or Buddhism, teaches it. Some believe in reincarnation because they want to believe that they will get a second chance on earth to be better people. But the Bible does not teach reincarnation. The Bible teaches that we have one life and then we face judgment.

KEY VERSE: *It is planned that men die only once. And after that comes judgment. (Hebrews 9:27)*

RELATED VERSES: *Luke 16:19-31*

RELATED QUESTIONS: *Does* born again *mean reincarnation? Is reincarnation replanting carnations? If you die, can you come back as a different person? What does the Bible say about reincarnation?*

NOTE TO PARENTS: *Some children misinterpret the term* born again *to mean reincarnation. You can explain that being born again means to be born into God's family, not to come back as a different person later. Being born again happens when we trust in Jesus Christ as Savior. It's not reincarnation.*

Q: WHAT'S A CASKET?

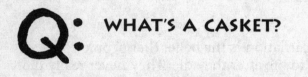

170

A: A casket is a metal or wooden box in which a dead body is placed. Usually a casket is buried in the ground in a cemetery. Putting a body in a casket is a very old custom and is a way of showing respect for the dead person. Also, it is part of the custom of mourning the person's death.

KEY VERSE: *It will be an honor to have you [Abraham] choose the finest of our tombs, so that you can bury [Sarah] there. (Genesis 23:6)*

RELATED VERSES: *Genesis 50:26; Amos 2:1; Mark 15:46; Romans 12:15*

RELATED QUESTIONS: *How can people be cremated? How can adults be cremated when they're so big?*

Q: WHY DO PEOPLE CRY AT FUNERALS?

171

A: People cry at funerals because they are very sad. They miss the person who has died. Even when people know that their family member or friend is now in heaven with Jesus, they cry because they miss their loved one. The purpose of funerals is to say good-bye to the dead person, to show respect for the person and his or her family, to cry and be sad, and to remember what the person meant to everyone.

KEY VERSES: *Tears came to Jesus' eyes. "They were close friends," the Jewish leaders said. "See how much he loved him." (John 11:35-36)*

RELATED VERSES: *Mark 5:38-39; Luke 7:11-15; Romans 12:15*

RELATED QUESTION: *Why do we have funerals?*

Q: WHY DO THEY PUT STONES ON PEOPLE'S GRAVES?

Rock vs. Paper →

R.I.P.

R.I.P

172

A: A gravestone or metal plate on a grave marks the place where the person's body is buried. After a person has died, friends and family will sometimes go to the cemetery, put flowers on the grave, and think about that person. The stone helps them find the grave. They can go there and remember the person instead of forgetting. Just think what it would be like if a family member was buried and no one marked where the grave was.

KEY VERSE: *The Lord buried [Moses] in a valley near Beth-peor in Moab. But no one knows the exact place. (Deuteronomy 34:6)*

RELATED VERSE: *Acts 13:36*

RELATED QUESTIONS: *Why do people talk to dead people at their graves? Why do people visit people's graves if their spirits have already gone to heaven?*

Q: WHY DO WE GIVE FLOWERS TO PEOPLE AFTER THEY HAVE DIED?

173

A: Many people bring flowers to funerals, wakes, and gravesides. It looks as though they are giving something to someone who can't enjoy the gift. Why would they do that? It is to show respect and to show that they miss the person. It's like saying, "I wish you were still here. I love you. I miss you." Also, flowers remind us of life. Most important, people give flowers to honor the person and the family of the person who has died. Flowers on a casket or on a grave say, "This person was important to me."

KEY VERSE: *When others are happy, be happy with them. If they are sad, share their sadness. (Romans 12:15)*

RELATED VERSES: *Isaiah 40:6; Amos 2:1; 1 Peter 1:24; 2:17*

Q: WILL I BE ABLE TO PLAY GAMES IN HEAVEN?

174

A: Heaven will be more exciting than you could possibly imagine. Will that mean playing lots of games? Probably not—you can get bored with games, and life in heaven will *never* be boring. You will never get tired of what you're doing there. The Bible says that you will always be happy in heaven. If you think games are fun, you should see what's coming next—it will be *much* better than playing games all the time.

It's OK if you don't understand this. Trying to understand life in heaven is like trying to understand how fun an amusement park will be before you get there. How can you really know what to expect? You can't. All you can do is hear the descriptions ("It's great! It's wonderful! You can ride on the SuperCollosalMachine!"). Until you go, you won't *really* be able to get excited about it. But once you're there, *wow!*

KEY VERSE: *We can see and understand only a little about God now. It is like we were looking at his reflection in a poor mirror. Someday we are going to see him face to face. Now all that I know is hazy and blurred. But then I will see everything clearly. (1 Corinthians 13:12)*

RELATED VERSES: *1 Corinthians 13:11-12; Revelation 4:8-11; 7:15-17; 22:3*

RELATED QUESTIONS: *Will there be lots and lots of toys in heaven? Will I still get to drive a car when I'm in heaven, or can you take a bus somewhere?*

NOTE TO PARENTS: *The tadpole analogy (see the next question) is useful for questions about boredom in heaven.*

Q: IN HEAVEN, WE DON'T JUST SING AND WORSHIP ALL DAY, DO WE?

JASON'S IMAGINATION

175

A: In heaven, we will be happy all the time. Heaven will be a place made just for us. We read in the Bible about angels singing and praising God day and night, and we can't imagine doing that all the time. But remember that they are singing because they are *glad*. They aren't bored, tired, or old. They are expressing happiness and joy. God is the happiest person in the universe, and living in heaven means being there with him doing the same thing. Life with God is happy, joyful, and cool.

Imagine that you're a tadpole. All your life you've lived only in the water. You know that someday you'll become a frog and you'll get to live on land. But until you become a frog, you will have no idea what life on land is like. And if anyone tries to explain it to you, it won't sound very appealing because there's no water and you can't swim. That's the way it is with heaven. Until we get to heaven, it will be hard for us to understand what's so great about it. But once we're there, we'll be perfect and we'll have new bodies, and that will make all the difference.

KEY VERSE: *Now I can sing glad praises to the Lord. I can sing instead of lying in silence in the grave. (Psalm 30:12)*

RELATED VERSES: *Psalm 61:8; 89:1; Isaiah 35:10; 51:11; 1 Corinthians 2:9; 13:12; Revelation 4:8-11; 7:15-17*

RELATED QUESTIONS: *Won't heaven be boring? Will I be bored in heaven?*

NOTE TO PARENTS: *Children can understand singing for joy by thinking of songs they sing when they're happy or celebrating. What they feel when singing those songs is like what they will feel in heaven—only better!*

Q: WHAT WILL I DO UP THERE WITH NO FRIENDS?

176

A: If your friends believe in Jesus, they will be in heaven with you, and you will have a *great* time together. Jesus is preparing a place for us; he won't keep us apart from each other. And we'll make new friends in heaven, too. If you aren't sure whether your friends will go to heaven, tell them about Jesus. If they put their faith in Christ, too, you will all be there together.

You don't have to worry—heaven *won't* be boring. Remember, God created butterflies, sunsets, electrical storms, mountains, the Grand Canyon, and all of nature. He will give us so much fun, beauty, and joy in heaven that we can hardly imagine it now.

KEY VERSES: *There are many homes in my Father's house. I am going to prepare a place for you. I will come again and take you to me. Then you will be with me where I am about to go. (John 14:2-3)*

RELATED VERSES: *1 Thessalonians 4:13-17*

RELATED QUESTIONS: *Who can I play with when I die? Will I be able to play with my friends up in heaven? Will I remember my family and friends in heaven? Will there be any stuffed animals? Is there going to be any paint in God's world? What happens when we go to heaven?*

Q: WILL I STILL HAVE FEELINGS IN HEAVEN?

177

A: Yes! People in heaven have lots of feelings—all good ones. People in heaven are filled with joy! You will be busy smiling, whistling, and singing for joy. When you are not doing that, you will be kicking your heels and jumping. Occasional high fives will interrupt the joviality. The timing will be perfect, and you'll love it. You will be happy because you will be with God and because all sin, death, and sadness will be gone forever. And think of the joy when you see your family and friends. Heaven will be a place of great joy and gladness—great feelings all around.

KEY VERSE: *You will give me back my life. You will give me great joy in your presence. (Acts 2:28)*

RELATED VERSES: *Jeremiah 31:13; Matthew 25:34; John 16:20-22*

Q: CAN WE STILL HAVE BIRTHDAYS IN HEAVEN?

JASON'S
IMAGINATION

178

A: The great thing about birthdays is the parties. In heaven, we won't grow old, but we will have lots of parties. The biggest party will be the celebration of "the wedding feast of the Lamb," when we celebrate our new life in heaven with Jesus. It will be ten times more fun than any birthday you've ever had.

The things we enjoy here on earth are like appetizers. They give us only a taste of what heaven will be like. The things you enjoy here on earth will only be better and greater in the presence of God.

KEY VERSE: *And the angel spoke to me. He said, "Blessed are those who are invited to the wedding feast of the Lamb." (Revelation 19:9)*

RELATED VERSES: *Isaiah 25:6-8*

NOTE TO PARENTS: *Heaven lacks a lot of the things that kids enjoy—toys, television, and games. This confuses many kids because they think they need these things to be happy. They don't realize that enjoyment of kid things depends on their being kids. In heaven they won't be kids anymore—they'll be perfect, so they'll enjoy different things. What will make us happy in heaven will match who we will be then, and that's something we can't see very well right now (1 Corinthians 13:12).*

Q: WILL YOU SEE YOUR GREAT-GREAT-GRANDPARENTS IN HEAVEN?

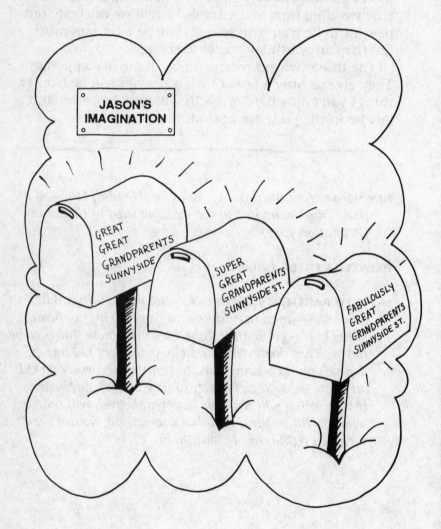

179

A: All people who have ever believed in Jesus, no matter how long ago, will be in heaven. If your great-great-grandparents believed in Jesus, they will be there. Even though you have never met your great-great-grandparents, you will be able to meet them there. But not every person who ever lived has believed, so not every person will be there.

KEY VERSE: *God has reserved for his children the priceless gift of eternal life. It is kept in Heaven for you. It is pure and spotless. It is beyond the reach of change and decay. (1 Peter 1:4)*

RELATED VERSES: *Romans 16:26; Hebrews 12:22-24; 1 Peter 1:3-5; 2 Peter 1:11; Revelation 7:9*

NOTE TO PARENTS: *This kind of question could mean, "In heaven, will we see all people who have ever lived?" The answer is, "No, only those who have trusted in Christ as Savior." Or it could mean that your child is curious about past relatives whom he or she has never met. If great-great-grandparents and others were believers, this would be a great time to tell about your family's heritage of faith.*

Q: WILL WE LOOK LIKE WE DO NOW IN HEAVEN?

HOUSE
OF
MIRRORS

180

A:

No one knows *exactly* what we will look like in heaven, but the Bible makes it clear that we will have new bodies—resurrected and perfect bodies. We will be different, but we surely won't be strangers to each other. We will be able to recognize each other and enjoy each other's company, just as we do here on earth—except it will be better because we'll never fight!

KEY VERSE: *When [Christ] comes back, he will change these dying bodies of ours. He will make them into glorious bodies like his own. (Philippians 3:21)*

RELATED VERSES: *Matthew 17:1-13; Luke 16:19-31; 1 Corinthians 15:35-58*

RELATED QUESTIONS: *Do you look like yourself in heaven? When people are dead, why don't they look like themselves? What will we look like in heaven?*

Q: WHEN WE GO TO HEAVEN, WILL WE GET SNARLS IN OUR HAIR?

181

A: Nope. Heaven is a place of happiness and joy—a place of no pain. We won't have irritations and frustrations. Also, we'll have new, "glorified" bodies. Our hair won't be the kind that snarls.

KEY VERSE: *Every human being has a body just like Adam's, made of dust. But all who become Christ's will have the same kind of body as his. It is a body from Heaven. (1 Corinthians 15:48)*

RELATED VERSES: *1 Corinthians 15:35-58; Revelation 21:4*

RELATED QUESTIONS: *If you just ask for something in heaven, will it just appear before you? Will there be any schools in heaven?*

Q: **WILL PEOPLE HAVE SCARS IN HEAVEN?**

182

A: In heaven, everyone will have new bodies, and no one will feel any pain. There will be no physical or mental disabilities. Everybody will be able to sing, think, talk, run, and play . . . without growing tired. People may have scars, but they won't look bad.

KEY VERSE: *The bodies we have now shame us. They become sick and die. But they will be full of glory when we come back to life again. Yes, they are weak, dying bodies now. But when we live again they will be strong. (1 Corinthians 15:43)*

RELATED VERSES: *Luke 24:40; John 20:27; 1 Corinthians 15:35-53; 2 Corinthians 4:16–5:5; Revelation 21:4*

NOTE TO PARENTS: *The pattern for heaven should be our pattern, too: to affirm people as they are, not reject them for being different or "imperfect."*

Q: ARE THERE ANIMALS IN HEAVEN?

183

A: When God creates the new heaven and the new earth, he will make all of creation new, and that includes the animal kingdom. But keep in mind that the animals won't be just like they are here on earth. They won't be dangerous. They won't attack people or be afraid of us. And all of them will get along with each other; they won't need to eat other animals. The Bible also says there will be plant life in heaven, such as trees. And perhaps best of all, no one will be allergic to any of it—dogs, cats, pollen, or anything!

KEY VERSE: *In that day the wolf and the lamb will lie down together. And the leopard and goats will be at peace. (Isaiah 11:6)*

RELATED VERSES: *Isaiah 11:6-9; 55:12-13; Romans 8:18-21; Revelation 22:2*

RELATED QUESTIONS: *If God made everything, will there be dragons in heaven? Will only dogs go to heaven? Will insects go to heaven? Will there be any lizards in heaven? Will there be any birds in the new world? Will my pet go to heaven when it dies? Will there be any feathers and ducks in heaven? Will there be any reindeers in heaven? Are there going to be any mice or frogs?*

NOTE TO PARENTS: *There is no evidence in the Bible that animals will be resurrected. So we don't really know if a child's pet will be in heaven with him or her. All we know is that we will have in heaven whatever we need to be happy.*

Q: WILL WE EAT IN HEAVEN?

JASON'S IMAGINATION

184

A: We will be *able* to eat in heaven, but we won't *have* to eat to live, as we do on earth. Jesus said he would eat with his people there. But no one in heaven will ever go hungry.

KEY VERSE: *Here in Jerusalem the Lord Almighty will spread a great feast. It will be for everyone around the world. It will be a tasty feast of good food. There will be clear, well-aged wine and choice beef. (Isaiah 25:6)*

RELATED VERSE: *Matthew 26:29*

RELATED QUESTIONS: *Does heaven have hotels or inns? What do angels eat? Are angels fat? Is there junk food up in heaven? What does Jesus eat in heaven? Will there be restaurants to eat at in heaven? Are there food fights in heaven? Does heaven have sections for candy, one for cereal, etc.? Will they have Kool-Aid in heaven?*

Q: WILL WE WEAR CLOTHES IN HEAVEN?

185

A: The Bible says that people will wear clothes in heaven—dazzling white robes. But people won't wear clothes for the same reasons that they wear them here. On earth, people wear clothes to protect them from bad weather, to cover their nakedness, and to impress other people. We won't need clothes to protect us from the cold because it won't be cold. We won't need raincoats because it won't be stormy. And we won't need special designer clothes because we won't need to show off.

KEY VERSE: *I saw a great crowd, too big to count. They were from all nations and lands and languages. I saw them standing in front of the throne and before the Lamb. They were dressed in white. And they had palm branches in their hands. (Revelation 7:9)*

RELATED VERSES: *Mark 9:3; Revelation 3:18; 4:4*

RELATED QUESTIONS: *Will people be naked in heaven? Do angels have to buy things? Why are some angels naked?*

186

A: Whenever God creates a person, he creates a new soul, a new person who never existed before. Babies do not live in heaven waiting to be born here on earth. The starting place for every person is right inside the mother's womb.

KEY VERSE: *You made all the parts of my body. You put them together in my mother's womb. (Psalm 139:13)*

RELATED VERSES: *Genesis 1:27-28; 2:7; 1 Corinthians 11:8*

Q: DO PEOPLE WALK IN HEAVEN, OR DO THEY FLY TO WHERE THEY NEED TO BE?

187

A: We don't know for sure how people get around in heaven. The Bible does say that angels fly, but it never says that people have wings or that they fly around, not even in heaven. Usually descriptions of people in heaven talk about them standing or walking.

KEY VERSE: *I saw a great crowd, too big to count. They were from all nations and lands and languages. I saw them standing in front of the throne and before the Lamb. They were dressed in white. And they had palm branches in their hands. (Revelation 7:9)*

RELATED VERSE: *Revelation 14:6*

Q: DOES JESUS COME INTO YOUR HOUSE IN HEAVEN FOR A VISIT?

188

A: Jesus always visits those who let him in. On earth, Jesus often visited his friends Mary, Martha, and Lazarus. In his early ministry, he went to a friend's wedding. And just before Jesus went to the cross, he told his disciples that he would eat and drink with them in heaven. Jesus will visit all of his friends in heaven, including you. Just think—we will finally get to see him face-to-face!

KEY VERSE: *Mark my [Jesus'] words. I will not drink wine again until I drink it with you in my Father's Kingdom. (Matthew 26:29)*

RELATED VERSES: *Mark 14:25; Luke 22:18; John 12:1-3; 14:2; 21:4-14; Revelation 3:20*

RELATED QUESTIONS: *Can you have a sleepover with God when you're in heaven? Will there be a lot of windows in our house? Will we be able to walk through walls when we're in heaven? Do they have furniture in heaven?*

NOTE TO PARENTS: *Above all else, God seeks a relationship with us. That is why he created us, that is why he sent his Son to die for us, and that is why he is preparing a place for us. Remind your child that being with us matters very much to God—now, as well as in heaven.*

Q: WHAT WOULD HAPPEN IF I ACCIDENTALLY SWORE IN HEAVEN?

JASON'S IMAGINATION

189

A: You will *never* accidentally swear in heaven, because no one in heaven can sin. You cannot do wrong in God's presence. Jesus will make all of his people perfect, like himself, so you won't *want* to sin. Messing up is one thing you'll never have to worry about again.

KEY VERSE: *Yes, dear friends, we are already God's children. We can't imagine what it is going to be like later on. But we do know that when he comes we will be like him. We shall see him as he really is. (1 John 3:2)*

RELATED VERSE: *1 Corinthians 13:12*

RELATED QUESTIONS: *Is heaven as nice as we think? If I swear, will I go to hell when I die?*

NOTE TO PARENTS: *The real concern here may be that your children do not feel they are good enough to get into heaven. Assure them that if they believe in Jesus as their Savior, they will go to heaven. Also, as they pray and trust God to help them, they will become more like Jesus.*

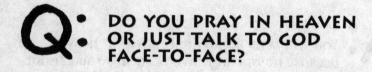

Q: DO YOU PRAY IN HEAVEN OR JUST TALK TO GOD FACE-TO-FACE?

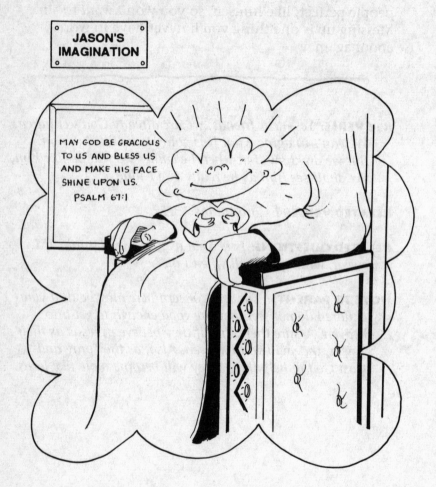

190

A: We will be able to talk to God face-to-face. (Moses talked with God face-to-face on earth, but that was unusual.) Remember, God wants to be our friend. Right now we are separated a little, and we have to pray to talk to God. But that relationship will be made perfect in heaven. Finally we will be able to go right up to God and talk to him, just as we have always wanted to do. In heaven, we will see God just as he is.

KEY VERSE: *We can see and understand only a little about God now. It is like we were looking at his reflection in a poor mirror. Someday we are going to see him face to face. Now all that I know is hazy and blurred. But then I will see everything clearly. I will see as clearly as God sees into my heart right now. (1 Corinthians 13:12)*

RELATED VERSES: *Exodus 33:11; Acts 7:56-59; 1 Thessalonians 5:10; Revelation 4:8-11; 21:3-4*

RELATED QUESTIONS: *Will we be able to see God when we are in heaven? Will I get to see and be with Jesus in heaven? When you're visiting with Jesus in heaven, does he know what you're going to say before you say it?*

Q: WILL WE LIVE WITH ANGELS IN HEAVEN?

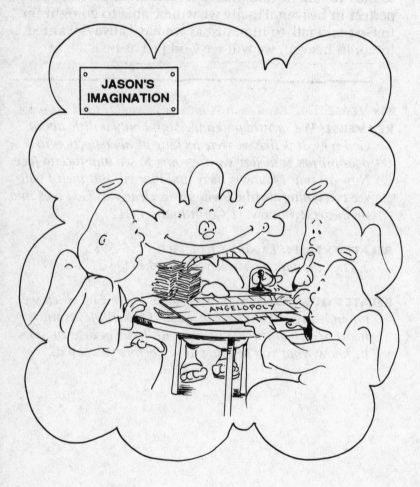

JASON'S IMAGINATION

ANGELOPOLY

191

A: We will live with God and the angels. But the angels will not be equal to us there. The angels are God's messengers, his servants. Part of the angels' job is to help us here on earth. Our friends and family in heaven will be the people we have known here on earth and other Christians who have died. Remember, angels aren't people; they're God's servants.

KEY VERSE: *Don't you know that we will judge the angels in Heaven? (1 Corinthians 6:3)*

RELATED VERSES: *John 14:3; Hebrews 1:14*

RELATED QUESTION: *Who will live with angels in heaven?*

Q: WILL THERE BE ANY CHURCH IN HEAVEN?

192

A: There will be no churches or temples in heaven because we won't need them. We will be right there in the presence of God. We will be perfect and sinless, so we won't need to go to Sunday school to learn about God or about how to obey him. We won't need worship leaders because we will worship just by being there. We will know God and see him face-to-face.

KEY VERSE: *No temple could be seen in the city. Why? Because the Lord God Almighty and the Lamb are worshiped in it everywhere. (Revelation 21:22)*

RELATED VERSES: *1 Corinthians 13:12; Revelation 21:1–22:17*

NOTE TO PARENTS: *After a question like this, explain the purpose of the church on earth and why it is necessary to attend. Also, if your child views church as boring, he may be asking if heaven is boring. Assure him that heaven is a wonderful, exciting place.*

Q: WILL GOD BE WITH ME ALL THE TIME IN HEAVEN?

193

A: Yes! In heaven, you will get to go right up to God and talk to him. God will be with you all the time, and you will be with him. God will be your friend, and you will be his. Getting to be with God will be one of heaven's greatest joys.

KEY VERSE: *I heard a loud shout from the throne. It was saying, "Look, the home of God is now among men. He will live with them and they will be his people. Yes, God himself will be among them." (Revelation 21:3)*

RELATED VERSES: *1 Corinthians 13:12; 2 Corinthians 5:8*

RELATED QUESTION: *Can God be my best friend?*

Q: WILL THERE BE A BIBLE "HALL OF FAME" IN HEAVEN?

194

A: Some people think that heaven is just like earth, with shopping malls, schools, athletic stadiums, and airports. But heaven is very different from earth. The focus in heaven is on God, not people. We will praise and worship God because no one's fame can compare with his.

People *will* be honored in heaven, however. The Bible says that believers will receive rewards for their good deeds. The greatest reward, of course, is just getting there. God gives salvation—a free gift made possible by Jesus' death on the cross—to all who put their faith in Christ. He will give other rewards to every believer who does good deeds for God on earth. Everyone's service will be rewarded.

KEY VERSE: *See, I am coming soon, and my reward is with me. I will repay everyone according to the deeds he has done. (Revelation 22:12)*

RELATED VERSES: *Romans 5:1; 14:12; 1 Corinthians 3:9-15; 9:16-27; 2 Corinthians 5:10; Revelation 3:5*

RELATED QUESTIONS: *Does God give out awards in heaven? Will there be a president in heaven?*

NOTE TO PARENTS: *It's easy to confuse rewards for good service with salvation by works. We receive our salvation by faith, not good deeds!*

Q: CAN WE SEE PEOPLE FROM THE BIBLE IN HEAVEN?

JASON'S IMAGINATION

SAMSON

195

A: Everyone who has ever trusted in Christ for salvation will be in heaven, and that includes all the Bible people who ever believed. You will get to know them, too. They can be your new friends!

KEY VERSE: *God wanted them [his people in the Bible] to wait and share the better rewards that were prepared for us. (Hebrews 11:40)*

RELATED VERSES: *2 Samuel 12:22-23; Matthew 17:3; Luke 23:43; Hebrews 12:1*

NOTE TO PARENTS: *When reading Bible stories, remind your children that the stories are true and that the Bible heroes are living now with God. This should help to make the stories more real.*

Q: WHY CAN'T I SEE JESUS NOW?

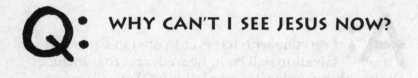

196

A: Jesus went back to heaven to be with his Father, but he has *not* forgotten about his people. In fact, he is preparing a place for all who believe in him, getting it ready for when they die and go to be with him. Also, Jesus is acting as our High Priest (like in the Old Testament)—whenever his people sin, he presents his own death as a payment so God can forgive them.

You may remember that the Bible calls Satan the Accuser. That's because he tells God the believers' faults to get God to reject his people. (There's an example in Job 1:6-11.) Whenever the devil accuses a believer, Jesus defends that person. We can't see Jesus now because it's not a part of God's plan.

Meanwhile, Jesus has not left his people alone. He has sent the Holy Spirit to be with them wherever they go. That's why Jesus said, "It is best for you that I go away" (John 16:7). When Jesus comes back, he will take all believers to live with him forever. Then you *will* be able to see Jesus in person.

KEY VERSE: *It is best for you that I [Jesus] go away. For if I don't, the Comforter won't come. If I do, he will. For I will send him to you. (John 16:7)*

RELATED VERSES: *Job 1:6-11; John 14:2-20, 28; Acts 1:9-11; 1 Corinthians 13:12*

RELATED QUESTIONS: *Why did God stop sending angels to people in visions? How come God had to use angels? Why do angels come to you and not God himself?*

Q: WHEN WILL THE WORLD END?

197

A: The world will not end until God is ready to take all believers home to heaven. It will happen when God decides that it is the right time. And no one knows when that time will come. Only God the Father knows. People who trust in God should not be afraid about the world coming to an end because it will be God's time of rescuing them from trouble and pain.

KEY VERSES: *Heaven and earth shall disappear. But my words stand sure forever. However, no one knows the day or hour when these things will happen. The angels in Heaven don't even know. I myself don't know. Only the Father knows. (Mark 13:31-32)*

RELATED VERSES: *Matthew 10:22; John 16:33; 2 Peter 3:10; Revelation 7:14-17*

RELATED QUESTION: *When is the world finished?*

Q: HOW WILL THE WORLD END?

198

A: The world will not end by an accident but by God's power. Right now God keeps the world safe from being destroyed. But someday, at the time he decides, God will burn up the world with fire. Then he will create a new heaven and a new earth, where all believers will live forever.

KEY VERSE: *The day of the Lord is surely coming. It will come as suddenly as a thief in the night. Then the heavens will pass away with a terrible noise. The heavenly bodies will disappear in fire [after we are gone]. The earth and everything on it will be burned up. (2 Peter 3:10)*

RELATED VERSES: *Mark 13:7; 2 Peter 3:10-14*

RELATED QUESTION: *Will God burn up the world?*

Q: IF JESUS HAS ALREADY WON, WHY IS EVERYONE STILL FIGHTING?

199

A: Jesus won over sin and death when he rose from the dead. But some people still sin and fight because they don't love or follow Jesus. Jesus is waiting for them to change their minds and follow him. As Jesus waits, they do what their sinful desires tell them to—they sin and fight. Satan has not surrendered, and he still tries to trick people. Jesus hasn't come back yet because he loves us all and wants many more people to trust in him as Savior so they can be saved from hell and go to heaven.

Jesus has won over sin and death, but he won't *make* us live at peace with each other. The more we love him, the more we learn to live at peace and not fight.

KEY VERSE: *When you understand you are useless before the Lord, he will lift you up. He will encourage and help you. (James 4:10)*

RELATED VERSES: *James 3:16; 4:1-6; 2 Peter 3:9-15*

RELATED QUESTION: *Why hasn't Jesus come back yet?*

Q: WHAT HAPPENS TO THE BAD PEOPLE WHEN JESUS COMES BACK?

200

A: When Jesus comes back to earth, people who know Jesus will be glad. But people who don't know Jesus will be very sad and afraid because they will be judged for their sin. Those who have not believed in Jesus as their Savior will be punished and sent to hell, far away from God. That is one of the reasons God urges us to tell our friends about Jesus—so they can join us and God in heaven.

KEY VERSE: *[Nonbelievers] will be punished in everlasting hell. They will be forever separated from the Lord. They will never see the glory of his power. (2 Thessalonians 1:9)*

RELATED VERSES: *1 Corinthians 4:5; 2 Thessalonians 1:6-10; 2 Timothy 4:1; Jude 1:14-15; Revelation 20:11-15*

RELATED QUESTIONS: *Will everyone see Jesus when he comes back? Does God ever fight back? Does God fight everyone that is or was bad? Will the bad people be crushed when the new Jerusalem lands on them?*

NOTE TO PARENTS: *Be careful not to divide the world between "good people" and "bad people." Many so-called good people don't trust in Christ, and they will be judged for their sin. Meanwhile, some Christians do bad things, yet they will receive eternal life because of their faith in Christ.*

Q: HOW CAN GOD MOVE A WHOLE CITY DOWN TO EARTH?

201

A: The apostle John had a vision of God bringing the new Jerusalem, the Holy City, down from heaven. We don't know exactly how this will work, but it will happen—God can do anything. He created all the stars and planets, as well as all the plants, animals, and human beings. He can certainly create a new city and bring it to earth.

KEY VERSE: *And I, John, saw the Holy City, the new Jerusalem. It was coming down from God out of Heaven. (Revelation 21:2)*

RELATED VERSE: *Revelation 3:12*

RELATED QUESTION: *What's going to happen to the houses and buildings on earth when the new Jerusalem comes?*

Q: WHEN JESUS COMES TO GET US, WHAT WILL HAPPEN TO EARTH AND EVERYONE ELSE?

202

A: When Jesus comes back to rescue all who believe in him, several things will happen: (1) Jesus will bring life on earth to an end. (2) Jesus will judge everyone. (3) Jesus will create a new heaven and new earth. (4) We will begin eternal life with God. (5) The devil, his demons, and all unbelievers will begin their eternal death in hell.

KEY VERSE: *Then I saw a new earth and a new Heaven. The first earth and Heaven had disappeared. And there was no more sea. (Revelation 21:1)*

RELATED VERSES: *1 Thessalonians 4:16-17; 2 Peter 3:10; Revelation 21:1–22:21*

RELATED QUESTIONS: *In the new Jerusalem will I be Jewish? Will God still be making things in heaven? Who's the archangel who blows the trumpet? Jesus said he wouldn't destroy the earth by rain anymore, but could he destroy it by fire?*

Q: WHEN WILL JESUS COME BACK?

203

A: No one knows when Jesus will come back, not even the angels. God has chosen not to tell us. God has also warned us not to listen to people who say they know when Jesus will return. The day of Christ's return will come "like a thief in the night," when no one is expecting it. People who say they know the date of Christ's return are just trying to trick you. You don't have to worry about missing Jesus when he returns. When Jesus comes back, it will be obvious to everyone. All people all over the world will know.

KEY VERSE: *No one knows the date and hour when the end will be. Not even the angels know this. No, not even God's Son knows this. Only the Father knows. (Matthew 24:36)*

RELATED VERSES: *Matthew 24:23-24, 36-44; Luke 21:8-9; 1 Thessalonians 5:1-11; 2 Thessalonians 2:1-6; 1 Peter 4:7*

RELATED QUESTIONS: *When will the world see God? Will Jesus be able to see everyone at once when he comes back? Does Jesus know when he's coming back? Will everyone see Jesus when he comes back? How could we see Jesus if he comes back on the other side of the earth? Will we hear something when Jesus comes back so we'll know to look up in the sky?*

Q: WOULD GOD MAKE A FRIENDLY GHOST LIKE CASPER?

204

A: No. Some people in the Bible thought they saw a ghost (a spirit) at times. When the disciples saw Jesus walking on the water, they thought he was a ghost. When an angel freed Peter from prison and his friend Rhoda saw him, she thought she was seeing "his angel." When Jesus appeared to his disciples after he rose from the dead, he said he was not a ghost. And some Bible translations use the word *ghost* to mean "spirit." But the Bible does *not* teach that spirits fly around visiting people. Many people have believed that after death, people come back as ghosts. But that's not taught in the Bible at all.

Some people call the Holy Spirit the Holy Ghost. When Jesus left the earth, he sent the Holy Spirit to live within us. He is the one who comforts, guides, and protects us.

KEY VERSE: *Then the Father will send the Comforter to you. The Comforter is the Holy Spirit. He will teach you much. And he will remind you of everything I myself have told you. (John 14:26)*

RELATED VERSES: *Matthew 14:26; Luke 24:39; John 14:15-26; Acts 12:1-19*

RELATED QUESTIONS: *Did God make ghosts? Can people come back from heaven to visit earth?*

Q: WHY DO SOME PEOPLE BELIEVE IN GHOSTS?

BOO!

205

A: A ghost is a disembodied spirit—the spirit of a person separated from the body. Some people believe in ghosts because they have heard about them on television shows, in movies, and in cartoons, and because many other people believe in ghosts. Some people believe in them because they have had strange experiences that they can't explain, and they figure that ghosts are the only answer.

The Bible gives no evidence that people come back to earth without their bodies. When you die, God takes your spirit from earth forever—believers into God's presence, unbelievers to a place of suffering. People do not come back as ghosts.

KEY VERSE: *It is planned that men die only once. And after that comes judgment. (Hebrews 9:27)*

RELATED VERSES: *Matthew 14:26-27; Luke 16:19-31; 24:37-39*

RELATED QUESTIONS: *When you are dead and you're up in heaven, could you talk to somebody on earth still? How can people come back from heaven when the doctors bring them back to life? If someone has a heart attack and dies and goes to heaven for a couple seconds and then comes back again, is it because the doctor saves him? Can people come back from heaven to visit earth?*

Q: WHY DID SAUL GO TO A FORTUNE-TELLER?

A: King Saul went to see a medium, or fortune-teller, because he was desperate. He did not trust in God to lead him. Saul wanted to find out things that he didn't have a right to know. In the law, God had told his people that they should never get involved with witchcraft, mediums, and fortune-tellers. Saul disobeyed God and did it anyway.

KEY VERSE: *Saul then ordered his aides to try to find a medium. He wanted to ask her what to do. (1 Samuel 28:7)*

RELATED VERSES: *Deuteronomy 18:10-11; 1 Samuel 28:3-25; Acts 16:16*

RELATED QUESTIONS: *How can people see things in crystal balls? Does celebrating Halloween make God unhappy? Is a séance when a dead person talks at their own funeral?*

NOTE TO PARENTS: *Dabbling in the occult is not a harmless pastime. Satan and demons are real beings that can influence the physical world, and occult practices only invite them to do so. Don't have Ouija boards, tarot cards, or other forms of occult fortune-telling in your home, and don't let your kids use them either. Remind your child that God loves us, has good plans for us, and has given us the Holy Spirit. He will give us wisdom if we ask him (James 1:5).*

Q: WHY DO SOME PEOPLE BELIEVE THAT TREES, PLANTS, AND ANIMALS HAVE SPIRITS?

WHOOOOO

207

A: Some people believe that trees, plants, and animals have spirits because they are confused. Plants and animals don't have spirits, but many false religions teach that they do. Only *people* have eternal souls.

At the same time, God does want us to respect the world he created. God created all living things, including plants and animals. The Bible says that all of nature groans under the weight of our sin. And some of the psalms in the Bible say, as a figure of speech, that the trees of the fields will clap their hands in praise of God. But plants and animals don't have spirits. And even more important to remember is that we are to worship only God, not anyone or anything else.

KEY VERSE: *Praise [God] for the growing fields. For they prove his greatness. Let the trees of the forest rustle with praise. (Psalm 96:12)*

RELATED VERSES: *Exodus 20:3-5; Isaiah 1:29; 55:12; 57:5-6; Hosea 4:13*

RELATED QUESTIONS: *When my pet dies, does it go to heaven or hell? Is the New Age movement when people move to a new place? What is the New Age movement?*

Q: WHY DO THEY PUT HOROSCOPES IN THE NEWSPAPER?

208

A: Newspapers print horoscopes because many people want to read them. And people read horoscopes because they believe that major parts of life are controlled by outside forces beyond their control. They look to the horoscopes for guidance.

Believers should not look to horoscopes for guidance. Only God controls what happens, and only God knows the future. If we need advice, we should do three things: (1) read the Bible, (2) talk to wise people (Proverbs 13:20), and (3) ask God for wisdom (James 1:5). If you are worried about the future, the best thing to do is to pray and tell God about your worries, ask him to take care of you, and trust him to do it (Philippians 4:6).

KEY VERSE: *[God's people] must not be serpent charmers, mediums, or wizards. They must never call forth the spirits of the dead. (Deuteronomy 18:11)*

RELATED VERSES: *Deuteronomy 18:10-13; 2 Kings 17:16-17; Psalm 147:4; Isaiah 34:4; Philippians 4:6; James 1:5; 1 Peter 5:7*

RELATED QUESTIONS: *Why do some people try to trick other people by saying they can tell fortunes? Is ESP some kind of tax?*

NOTE TO PARENTS: *Horoscopes are closely related to occult practices. It's better to turn to God for guidance, wisdom, and assurance for the future.*

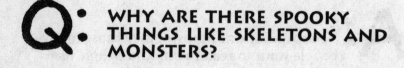

Q: WHY ARE THERE SPOOKY THINGS LIKE SKELETONS AND MONSTERS?

209

A: Some people like to be frightened by funny skeletons and make-believe monsters. And they like scaring others, especially at Halloween. But you don't have to be afraid of ghosts and goblins because they aren't real. Besides, God is with you and will take care of you. Keep trusting in him to protect you.

KEY VERSE: *Be strong! Be brave! Do not be afraid of them! For the Lord your God will be with you. He will neither fail you nor forsake you. (Deuteronomy 31:6)*

RELATED VERSES: *Matthew 28:20; Luke 12:4-5; John 16:33*

RELATED QUESTIONS: *Are there such things as haunted houses? Are ghosts real? If ghosts are real, are they the devil's demons? Why are there monsters? Why is there Halloween?*

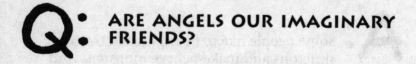

Q: ARE ANGELS OUR IMAGINARY FRIENDS?

210

A: Angels are real, not imaginary. Some people think they can talk to angels or that they have special angels who guide them. But the Bible teaches that angels are God's messengers—they serve him and do what he says. Often God tells them to help us. But they're not our friends the way people are or even the way God can be. Angels are God's servants, not people's, but they are as real as God is.

KEY VERSE: *For the Lord saves those who respect him. The Angel of the Lord guards them. (Psalm 34:7)*

RELATED VERSE: *Hebrews 1:14*

RELATED QUESTION: *Can angels tell people about Jesus?*

NOTE TO PARENTS: *A lot of children go through stages when they have imaginary friends, and many children may believe these friends are angels. This can be an ideal time to introduce them to a Friend who will always be with them—Jesus.*

Q: IF I DIE WHEN I'M A KID, WILL I MISS OUT ON DOING FUN THINGS ON EARTH?

JASON'S
IMAGINATION

211

A: When people die, their life on earth ends. That's true no matter how young or old a person is when he or she dies. But do these people miss their "fun" on earth? Are they up in heaven being sad about all the fun things they didn't get to do? Not at all! Living in the presence of God is the most enjoyable thing a person can do. It is what we were created for.

Don't worry—God has a wonderful plan for your life here on earth. Enjoy the life God has given you. You won't be sorry you went to heaven when the time comes for you to go!

KEY VERSES: *Sometimes I want to live, and at other times I don't. For I long to go and be with Christ. How much happier for me than being here! But I can be of more help to you by staying! (Philippians 1:23-24)*

RELATED VERSES: *Mark 12:25; Philippians 1:21-24*

RELATED QUESTIONS: *Will there be candy and television in heaven? Do they have video games in heaven? Do I get to stay up and not go to bed in heaven? Will there be Legos in heaven? If you die when you're a kid and go to heaven, can you get married? Will there be cartoons in heaven?*